EDMUND SPENSER

# Selected Poetry

# Crofts Classics

GENERAL EDITORS

Samuel H. Beer, *Harvard University*

O. B. Hardison, Jr., *The Folger Shakespeare Library*

John Simon

# EDMUND SPENSER

# *Selected Poetry*

EDITED BY

**A. Kent Hieatt**

AND

**Constance Hieatt**

THE UNIVERSITY OF WESTERN ONTARIO

New York

APPLETON-CENTURY-CROFTS

Educational Division

MEREDITH CORPORATION

# contents

# introduction

A surprising feature of Edmund Spenser's poetry is its
intellectual range. Some of his poetic narratives dramatize
a single idea—the need for a saving graciousness in social
intercourse, for example. More often, they examine the re-
lation between two ideas: of duty to pleasure, of the un-
committed life to goal-conscious activism, of our separate
existence to authority, of love to the other forces binding
us together, of marriage to religion, of violence to sexuality,
or of our lives to the pulse of the universe.

Much of what Spenser conveys to us about these and
other subjects is a blending of generally received opinions,
but it is a vital point for him and for us that he embodies
these ideas in the language and the fictional narrative of
poetry. One of his basic assumptions, shared by others of
his time, was that wisdom is stamped with ultimate validity
only when it is given poetic embodiment. Indeed, poetic
creations were often thought of during the Renaissance as
second only to sacred writ. Spenser, in his own eclogue
"October," and Spenser's highly placed friend Sir Philip
Sidney, in his Apology for Poetry, both say that in an im-
portant sense poets are godlike: each poet creates his own
world as God created ours. Because he is thus divinely in-
spired, a true poet with the right audience does not need
the resources of either physical compulsion or theatrical
argument to move men to good action; he can persuade
them by the invented actions of his poetic world, which
are as concrete and as moving as the actions and history
of the world we know (and far more directly edifying).

Given so serious a conception of the poetic calling,
aspiring poets like Spenser apparently conceived of their
poetic lives in terms of a long apprenticeship, in which
they would rise only gradually to the composition of the
highest forms of poetic narrative. For this program, their
central and original model was the career of the Roman

poet Vergil. Like Vergil's early works (e.g., the Bucolics), Spenser's first major work, The Shepherds' Calendar, belongs to the genre of poetry called pastoral. In this kind of poetry the most humble but apparently least trammeled of callings, that of shepherds, is made to display a simplicity and directness of spirit that the sophisticated and inhibited reader is presumed to have lost. The emphasis of pastoral poetry has usually been on this stance of innocent directness, not on what shepherds are really like.

The Calendar embodies this tradition in the form of twelve compositions, or eclogues, named after the months. Sometimes the shepherds of pastoral, accompanying their songs on oaten pipes, represent paradoxically the poets of more sophisticated society, to whose notions they are made to give a free and picturesque symbolic representation. In "October" the two shepherds Cuddie and Piers outline the calling of the poet much as it has already been described.

As the divinely inspired seer and teacher of mankind, the poet should advance from composing the lower kinds of poetry, such as the pastoral, to the warlike epic (as Vergil had done in the Aeneid and as Spenser was to do in The Faerie Queene). Indeed, beyond these the poet should ascend to sacred verse (as Spenser was to do in The Hymn of Heavenly Love and The Hymn of Heavenly Beauty), and to that inspired frenzy associated by both Renaissance writers and the ancients with Dionysus, the god of wine, whose festivals were the origins of Greek drama.

One of the reasons for escaping into sacred verse, according to Cuddie and Piers, is the decline of the world from an earlier and more perfect time. Now, says Cuddie, defective audiences and defective poets appreciate only ribald rhymes, not true poetry. One should not take this pessimism with complete seriousness. Spenser no doubt had his black moods, but like other Renaissance poets he was interested in finding fit expression for certain traditional rather than personal attitudes; and deprecation of the present age is a literary tradition as old as Hesiod.

The writing and publication of The Shepherds' Calendar allowed Spenser to think of himself as an English Vergil in more ways than we have indicated. Vergil and Spenser each looked back upon poetic predecessors, yet each wrote early enough in the development of his own language to shape and define that language as a literary instrument. As Vergil had done for Latin, so Spenser hoped to do for English; he hoped to create works that would make the language known for ages to come as a spring of divinely inspired utterance. In fact, at the time of its publication (1579), The Shepherds' Calendar was a major triumph in English letters. Its virtuosity in the use of stanzaic forms, its adept control of various meters, and its ability to stand comparison with the best Continental models must have seemed even more remarkable then than they now do. At that time, the English could look back on only one well-known and incontestably first-rate poet, Geoffrey Chaucer. English speech, however, had changed so much in the nearly one hundred and eighty years since Chaucer's death that his verses already sounded uncouth. The works of Sidney, Marlowe, Shakespeare, Jonson, and the other great Elizabethans were either not written or not yet published. Spenser's preeminence was immediately recognized, and the subsequent appearance of The Faerie Queene established him as the national poet of his time.

Spenser's language differs in one respect from that of other Elizabethan poets. He self-consciously created a literary speech by attempting to maintain verbal and lexical continuity with earlier English writers such as Chaucer. From them he borrowed many words and word meanings not current in his own time. The effect of this archaism is exaggerated in The Shepherds' Calendar: following a long-standing tradition, he established the rusticity of his shepherds by assigning them a rough-hewn, somewhat outlandish vocabulary. Spenser may have pursued a literary speech rooted in earlier English traditions more determinedly when he was young than he did later, but he did continue to use archaic turns of expression throughout his writing career. Consequently, except for his large band of imitators, other Elizabethan poets often sound more colloquial than Spenser. It needs to be noted, however, that judiciously used archaisms (in religious contexts, for instance) are a proved means for suggesting the language of beings other and better than our everyday selves. Also, even though the language Spenser created for himself may at first reading show a loss of flexibility and some limitation of emotional range, it often proves on inspection to be surprisingly direct.

After the publication of the Calendar, it was natural that Spenser should have dreamed of joining the company of those most revered poets each of whom had crowned his achievements by composing an epic. Such a narrative poem elevated from history into the eternity of divine poetry a nation, a society, a language, and—above all—a hero or heroes. Spenser's age thought that so-called heroic poems spoke not only of their ostensible subjects, but also, in ways hidden from the vulgar, of questions of the highest ethical and religious significance.

In Spenser's century Ariosto and Tasso had written what was considered the same kind of composition in Italian, and Ronsard had attempted one in French. Many other works—like the Aethiopica of Heliodorus (second or third century A.D.) and at least one version of the Arcadia by Sir Philip Sidney—were considered epics in the Renaissance although they would be considered unepical today and are not written in verse.*

Men of the Renaissance generally thought the epic to be the worthiest of all literary genres. Homer and Vergil provided the basic classical models for epic. The principal model for epic, however, was the Aeneid of Vergil, who had used it to immortalize an ideal hero, Aeneas, and to celebrate the Latin language and nation.

In the composition of his heroic poem, The Faerie Queene, Spenser followed both ancient and "modern" models. In the Aeneid Rome's beginnings, narrated through the exemplary deeds of Aeneas, form a context for praise of Vergil's emperor, Augustus, and for a vision of the perpetuity of Rome's imperial and peaceful rule. Something similar happens in Spenser's poem. His ultimate hero, who does not often appear in the incomplete Faerie Queene that Spenser left us, is King Arthur, familiar from medieval romances and known in supposedly historical accounts as an early preserver of Britain. Even more fully than Aeneas in Vergil's epic, Arthur would have been revealed in the complete Faerie Queene as a paragon of

---

* Etymologically a poem is a thing made or created—an artifact—not necessarily a composition in verse.

virtues. The poem, dedicated to Spenser's queen, Elizabeth I, postulates as does the Aeneid an uninterrupted and glorious perpetuity for the author's nation. Thus Elizabeth herself is idealized in her public role as Gloriana, the future spouse of Arthur, and in her private role as the virgin huntress Belphoebe.

Basically similar Vergilian influences had affected the two great heroic poems of sixteenth-century Italy, both of which also exerted strong influences on The Faerie Queene: Ariosto's Orlando Furioso (1532 in final form) and Torquato Tasso's Jerusalem Delivered (1580). Spenser sometimes follows the Orlando Furioso by interweaving quick-moving episodes from various knightly quests and adventures in a seriocomic tapestry of magic, of mythical beings, and of theatricality. This procedure may be traced in the present volume in the selections from Books I and III, ix–xi. The interweaving is also influenced by medieval romances, many of which Spenser used. From the Jerusalem Delivered he borrowed situations and characters, as well as a way of creating an atmosphere of high moral seriousness, distinctive of that Christian epic and appropriate to Spenser's own Christian concerns in The Faerie Queene. For the ultimate view of life presented by Spenser is always Christian, whatever allied views it may draw on.

In both of the Italian poems, and also in earlier English narrative poems like Chaucer's Troilus and Criseyde, Spenser observed the success of long narratives in stanzaic form, rather than in couplets, blank verse, or prose. The complex and difficult Faerie Queene stanza follows these precedents. It is formed of eight lines of iambic pentameter followed by one line of iambic hexameter, rhyming ababbcbcc. It has often been copied, for instance, in Keats' The Eve of St. Agnes and Byron's Childe Harold's Pilgrimage.

Commentaries on earlier heroic poems, both in Spenser's time and before, show that significances which are not obvious to us today were found in them. The story of Aeneas, for instance, was taken to show the development of the perfect man: each of his adventures signified allegorically the acquisition of a new virtue. If this general Renaissance tendency to find a pattern of higher meaning in every narrative was mistaken, then the mistake was a fortunate one for us. For under its influence Spenser made of his poem a highly allusive pattern of symbolic equivalences, and thereby gave to it an ethical and metaphysical multidimensionality that is his most original achievement. As he says in the "Letter to Raleigh" which prefaced the first three books of The Faerie Queene, each of his projected twelve books (we have six complete ones) was to embody a different virtue, each virtue with its separate hero or heroes. Sometimes exemplary episodes, narrated after the fashion of Ariosto or of medieval romance, carry the burden of meaning. At the same time, a mass of classical mythology, infused and transformed with countless accretions of meaning, may communicate the intended significance at either the level of straight narrative or that of simile and metaphor. A single episode may reinforce or contrast with others; names of persons and places may have several meanings.

One of Spenser's favorite and central devices, used in the fashion of Chaucer and other medieval allegorists, is an enclosed garden or temple or castle or island. This enclosed place is filled with supernally beautiful or especially significant objects and characters who set the governing pattern of meaning throughout a whole section or book of The Faerie Queene.

In the selections included here, which take place in a garden or another enclosed setting, Spenser also comes close to the thought of Chaucer and other medieval poets who speculated about the various forms of love. By different paths, Chaucer and Spenser reached perspectives on the world and its creatures which are largely Platonic, or Platonically Christian, in two senses. First, our universe, although it is an imperfect copy of the realm of ideal eternity, is the best one that can be made in time and space. From this fact certain moral consequences follow. Second, love, whose various forms are partly subject to our own choice, is the all-important element relating us to one another and to a higher perfection.

Three gardens of The Faerie Queene, all represented in the following pages, illustrate these points. The Bower of Bliss (II, xii) is the site of sexual love that is false and self-indulgent. It is destroyed by the hero of this Book of Temperance. The goddess Nature, who is traditionally concerned with maintaining the perpetual cycles of beautifully

recurring phenomena—whether the apparent orbiting of
the heavenly bodies around the earth, or, under direction
of her attendant Genius, the generating and reproducing
of man—does not rule the Bower of Bliss. On the con-
trary, an anti-Genius appears, and Nature and Art (arti-
fice) compete to produce a deceptive simulacrum of lasting
perfection, not perfection itself. A song about pleasure as
a rose that must be seized because it comes but once, sug-
gests the filching, opportunistic hedonism of the Bower.
In the second garden, the Garden of Adonis, sexual pleas-
ure exists not simply for its own sake but also for the per-
petually self-renewing cycles of life (III, vi). Here Nature
reigns, not Art. Human and animal lovers obey the in-
junction to wax and multiply in perpetual war against
Time; from this cyclical renewal arises the only true per-
fection that we, victims of mortality, can achieve here be-
low. In this garden Venus perpetually enjoys her Adonis,
a symbol of death and rebirth, and the geography of the
Mount of Venus suggests unashamedly the anatomy of
human reproduction. The third garden, the Isle of Venus
(IV, x), containing her temple, is presented in the Book
of Friendship. Nature and Art unite here in amity. To the
natural desires of lovers is added the gentle art by which
we become fellows one of another in spirit as well as in
flesh. Venus here is at one with loving Concord, who
binds the warring elements of the universe in ordered
harmony.

Chivalric adventure impinges on this allegorical scene.
Young Scudamore ("shield of Love") wins the shield
bearing Cupid's image—the mastering passion of love—
and with its help removes his beloved Amoret, protesting,
from the Temple of Venus. Although he finds her there,
she was raised in the Garden of Adonis, which first made
her a fit object for love. The rest of Amoret's story is told
in Book IV, i, 1–4, where the enchanter Busirane carries
her away from the drunken feast of her marriage, in the
Masque of Cupid (a procession of allegorical figures); and
in Book III, xi–xii. In the latter section Britomart, heroine
of the Book of Chastity, or true love, succeeds, as Scuda-
more cannot, in rescuing Amoret from the House of
Busirane. Scudamore here is fighting himself. To his mas-
culine tendency to passionate mastery the force of a total

and self-surrendering love, signified by Britomart, must be added to make the two lovers one.

Book VI, the Book of Courtesy, reverts to the pastoral mode of The Shepherds' Calendar. Here the knightly hero Sir Calidore comes from a center of power, giddy greatness, and heavy responsibility: the court of Gloriana, who is a type of Queen Elizabeth I. Sir Calidore's responsibility to Gloriana, the basis of his honor and career, demands planning, self-control, great effort, and much suffering. The duty laid upon him is the quest and capture of a ravening monster, the Blatant Beast, who endangers the commonweal. When his search brings him among simple shepherds and exposes him to the charms of the Pastorella, whom he supposes to be a shepherd maid, the pastoral paradoxes take over much as they do in Shakespeare's As You Like It. The innocent daily round, simple pleasures in picturesque surroundings, the immediate presence of incontestable beauty and innocence all strike Sir Calidore as vastly preferable to the suspect, sophisticated enjoyments of a court, to exhausting, continually keyed-up questing, and to the uncertain hope of a far-off exploit, for which he may lose all credit through smooth manipulations by the practiced timeservers found in any center of power. Sir Calidore's immediate feelings do not constitute Spenser's final answer to a problem that was a galling preoccupation for the author himself as servant of his queen, but, like other poets of his time, he found the most perfect objectification for such feelings in the pastoral form.

The scene viewed by Sir Calidore in the tenth canto of Book VI is also pastoral. Colin Clout, the shepherd-poet, plays on his pipes so that Venus' attendants, the three Graces, may dance in a circle around Colin's ladylove, a simple shepherd lass. They in turn are encircled by hundreds of other dancing graces. "Courtesy," then—the subject of Book VI—may come from "courts" and "civility" from "cities," but the source of true graciousness is really in nature, not art or artifice, and it is to be found among the lowly and rural, even though the Graces express the essence of an inherently social and urbane virtue in defining how we should behave in our exchanges with each other.

Colin Clout in fact stands for Spenser himself, domiciled in the rural (if not lowly) isolation of Ireland; Colin's lass is Spenser's own ladylove and later wife, whom he celebrates also in Amoretti and Epithalamion.

These two works, first published as a single book, had as their ostensible occasion Spenser's late courtship of, and marriage to, Elizabeth Boyle. Many Renaissance poets thought that the transient events of life and history could be raised to the eternal realm of poetry and thus immortalized. But the process of idealizing and typifying, by which one love relationship, for instance, became the perfect love relationship or the archetypal idea of such a state, obscured the given concrete personal or historical situation at its base. Also, according to the genre and intent of different poems, the same concrete situation might be reduced to different typical forms. Thus the Elizabeth Boyle glorified here is a more magnificent person than she is in her other, merely pastoral, apotheosis in The Faerie Queene, VI, x.

Amoretti is a sequence of sonnets in the so-called Petrarchan tradition. Accordingly, in a series of short lyrics of demanding form, Spenser orchestrates his unqualified devotion, his suffering, his unworthiness when compared with his imperious and perfect mistress, and the compulsion of her physical charms, straitly controlled by the purity of her admirable spirit. In the Platonizing tradition of the Renaissance he shows her beauty to be a revelation of the incorporeal beauty of the eternal, and he relates his and her possible love to divine—in fact Christian— love. Throughout, he writes in the figurative style appropriate to the form, using such metaphorical components as pearls, roses, fire, ice, Cupid's arrows, and his lady's eye beams. His sequence is more carefully organized than other sonneteers', and one suspects a complexly maintained balance between his own relation with Elizabeth Boyle and the idealized relation of lover and mistress in the poem.

The stanzaic form of these sonnets corresponds to the English or Shakespearean kind in containing three cross-rhymed quatrains followed by a couplet, but Spenser has marked it as his own by making the second rhyme of each quatrain the first rhyme of the quatrain immediately following: ababbcbccdcdee. This feature makes the Spenserian sonnet similar to the Faerie Queene stanza, which rhymes ababbcbcc.

Petrarch (1304–1374), the great Italian popularizer of the sonnet, included longer lyrics in his sonnet sequence. Usually these are in the canzone form, which, as Petrarch used it, often consists of a number of stanzas whose music depends on the interspersing of short lines among the long ones. At the end of the canzone he added a tornata, a short stanza in which the poet addresses his poem directly, calling it "canzone" (literally, "song"). Epithalamion, published at the end of Amoretti, conforms to the Petrarchan canzone in these respects. In another sense, Epithalamion belongs to the genre of epithalamium, or marriage poem, a traditional form since classical times. The poet of an epithalamium generally celebrates the whole of the marriage day in chronological sequence and alludes to the groom's ardor, the bride's beauty and maidenly diffidence, the preparations, the ceremony, the feast with its lusty excess, the coming to the bridal chamber, and the joys of the night. Venus and Hymen are usually invoked to insure a large progeny. In Epithalamion Spenser surpassed himself in exuberantly fitting a traditional poetic form to his own special case. Mainly because of its distinction of language and imagery and its sustained, evenly progressing emotional development, it has come to be recognized as one of the loveliest poems in the English language.

According to a theory further explained in the notes to the poem, Spenser also expresses in Epithalamion a correspondence similar to that discussed above in connection with the Garden of Adonis. Our cyclical efforts imitate Eternity by replacing, through love and marriage, our mortal selves with new selves; and the cycles of the heavens above us, also presided over by Nature, give us, by their perpetual returnings, a hint of the perfection of Eternity. Plato says in the Timaeus that God created these recurrences by number, and it is chiefly by number that Spenser expresses the analogy in the poem, which contains 24 stanzaic units, 365 long lines (i.e., pentameter and hexameter lines), and a division of stanzas into light and darkness corresponding to the actual division of hours at the time and place of the wedding. According to this theory,

the sun as well as the "song" is being addressed in the
tornata. The sun does not keep in "due time" with the
stars in the 24-hour apparent circuit of the day, but hangs
back slightly. For its deficiency, the sun yields, however, a
"recompense," in the sense that the hanging back is itself
the daily part of the sun's opposite, 365-day circle. By
means of this imperfection the other perfect cycle is
formed of the seasons and the year, through which human
life is sustained. The role of the sun here is perhaps paral-
leled in Amoret's having been miraculously begotten by
the sun (The Faerie Queene, III, vi, 7), and by the tra-
dition that Adonis in his cyclical return himself represents
the sun.

In addition, the first twelve stanzas of Epithalamion
may match the second twelve, stanza for stanza, so as to
create the seasonal divisions of the equinoxes (when hours
of light and darkness are equal) as well as the solstices.
The marriage day coincides with the summer solstice. Some
scholars, however, do not think that Spenser intended this
matching of stanzas.

The spelling and punctuation of the selections in this
edition have been modernized where such modernization
does not conflict with meter and rhyme. We believe that
those who come to a first reading of Spenser's work in its
original spelling and punctuation receive an unfair impres-
sion that he, unlike his contemporaries, is archaic and
quaint, because such beginners generally read those con-
temporaries (especially Shakespeare) in modernized form.
Our only emendation which does not, as far as we know,
appear in any other edition of Spenser is our solution to
the crux in The Faerie Queene, VI, x, 24, 7–8.

# principal dates in the life of Edmund Spenser

1554  Born in London. Family related to Spencers who were ennobled under Henry VII. Later attends Merchant Taylors' School.

1569  Publication of Spenser's translations of poems by Du Bellay and Petrarch. Enters Pembroke Hall, Cambridge, as sizar (poor student, not necessarily impoverished). While there forms friendship with the learned Gabriel Harvey. B.A. 1573. M.A. 1576.

1577  In Ireland (?).

1578  Secretary to John Young, bishop of Rochester, former master of Pembroke.

1579  In service with Earl of Leicester. Friendly with latter's nephew, Philip Sidney. Publishes *The Shepherds' Calendar* (dedicated to Sidney). Marries first wife (?).

1580  Goes to Ireland as secretary to Lord Grey, new Lord Deputy there. Drafts part of *The Faerie Queene*. Remains in Ireland for most of rest of life in official positions.

1582  Outlines *The Faerie Queene* to friend, Lodowick Bryskett.

1584(?)  Deputy to clerk of Council of Munster.

1588  In possession of castle of Kilcolman, County Cork, his permanent home.

1589  Sir Walter Ralegh admires *The Faerie Queene*. Spenser goes with him to London. Elizabeth I approves poem. Granted life annuity. Difference now (?) with Lord Burghley, chief minister.

1590  Publishes first three books of *The Faerie Queene*. Returns to Ireland.

1591   Publishes *Complaints,* a collection of various pieces mostly written much earlier (?).

1594   Marries Elizabeth Boyle.

1595   Publishes *Colin Clout's Come Home Again* (pastoral) and *Amoretti* and *Epithalamion.*

1596   In England. Publishes all six complete books of *The Faerie Queene;* also *Four Hymns* and *Prothalamion.*

1598   Sheriff of Cork. Kilcolman sacked in rebellion. Spenser comes to London with messages for Privy Council.

1599   Dies January 13. Buried in Westminster Abbey.

1609   *Two Cantos of Mutability* published (supposedly part of incomplete Book VII of *The Faerie Queene*).

# from The Shepherds' Calendar

## Eclogue X: October

### Argument

*In Cuddie is set out the perfect pattern of a poet, which finding no maintenance of his state and studies, complaineth of the contempt of poetry, and the causes thereof; specially having been in all ages, and even amongst the most barbarous, always of singular account and honor, and being indeed so worthy and commendable an art: or rather no art, but a divine gift and heavenly instinct not to be gotten by labor and learning, but adorned with both, and poured into the wit by . . . celestial inspiration . . .*

1

Piers:    Cuddie, for shame hold up thy heavy head,
        And let us cast with what delight to chase
        And weary this long lingering Phoebus' race.
        Whilom thou wont the shepherds' lads to lead,
        In rhymes, in riddles, and in bidding base:
        Now they in thee, and thou in sleep are dead.

---

**Argument** in the original edition an unknown "E. K." was the ostensible author of prose summaries ("arguments") for this and the other eclogues, and of a set of explanatory notes   1.5 **bidding base** the game of prisoner's base

1

2

*Cuddie:*   Piers, I have pipéd erst so long with pain
That all my oaten reeds been rent and wore,
And my poor muse hath spent her sparéd store,
Yet little good hath got, and much less gain.
Such pleasance makes the grasshopper so poor,
And lie so laid, when winter doth her strain;

3

The dapper ditties that I wont devise
To feed youth's fancy, and the flocking fry,
Delighten much: what I the bett for-thy?
They han the pleasure, I a slender prize.
I beat the bush, the birds to them do fly;
What good thereof to Cuddie can arise?

4

*Piers:*   Cuddie, the praise is better than the price,
The glory eke much greater than the gain:
O what an honor is it, to restrain
The lust of lawless youth with good advice,
Or prick them forth with pleasance of thy vein,
Whereto thou list their trainéd wills entice.

5

Soon as thou ginst to set thy notes in frame,
O how the rural routs to thee do cleave:
Seemest thou dost their soul of sense bereave,
All as the shepherd that did fetch his dame
From Pluto's baleful bower withouten leave:
His music's might the hellish hound did tame.

6

*Cuddie:*   So praisen babes the peacock's spotted train,
And wondren at bright Argus' blazing eye:

2.1 **erst** before   .5 **pleasance** pleasure   .6 **laid** prostrated
**strain** constrain   3.2 **fry** young people   .3 **bett** better **for-thy** for that, therefore   .4 **han** have   4.6 **trainéd** entrained, captive   5.1 **ginst** begin[est]   .2 **routs** bands, companies   .4 **shepherd . . . dame** Orpheus and Eurydice   6.2 **Argus' blazing eye** spots on the peacock's tail, said in classical myth to be the eyes of Argus

But who rewards him ere the more for-thy,
Or feeds him once the fuller by a grain?
Sike praise is smoke, that sheddeth in the sky;
Sike words been wind, and wasten soon in vain.


7

*Piers:*   Abandon then the base and viler clown;
Lift up thyself out of the lowly dust,
And sing of bloody Mars, of wars, of jousts;
Turn thee to those that wield the awful crown,
To 'doubted knights, whose woundless armor
    rusts,
And helms unbruiséd waxen daily brown.


8

There may the muse display her fluttering wing,
And stretch herself at large from east to west:
Whether thou list in fair Eliza rest,
Or if thee please in bigger notes to sing,
Advance the worthy whom she loveth best,
That first the white bear to the stake did bring.


9

And when the stubborn stroke of stronger
    stounds
Has somewhat slacked the tenor of thy string,
Of love and lustihead tho mayst thou sing,
And carol loud and lead the miller's round,
Al were Eliza one of thilke same ring.
So mought our Cuddie's name to heaven ring.


10

*Cuddie:*   Indeed the Romish Tityrus, I hear,
Through his Maecenas left his oaten reed,
Whereon he erst had taught his flocks to feed,

.5 **sike** such  **sheddeth** scatters  7.5 **'doubted** redoubted  .6
**brown** tarnished  8.3 **Eliza** Queen Elizabeth I  .5 **worthy**
Earl of Leicester  .6 **white bear** Leicester's arms  9.1 **stounds**
blows  .3 **lustihead** lustiness (-hood)  **tho** then  .4 **miller's**
**round** a dance  .5 **al** even if  **thilke** this  .6 **mought** might
10.1 **Tityrus** Vergil, lines below refer to his *Eclogues, Georgics,*
and *Aeneid*  .2 **Maecenas** Roman patron of poets

And labored lands to yield the timely ear,
And eft did sing of wars and deadly dread,
So as the heavens did quake his verse to hear.

11
But ah, Maecenas is y-clad in clay,
And great Augustus long ago is dead:
And all the worthies liggen wrapped in lead
That matter made for poets on to play:
For, ever, who in derring-do were dread,
The lofty verse of them was lovéd aye.

12
But after virtue gan for age to stoop,
And mighty manhood brought a-bed of Ease,
The vaunting poets found naught worth a pease
To put in press among the learned troop.
Tho gan the streams of flowing wits to cease,
And sunbright honor penned in shameful coop.

13
And if that any buds of poesie
Yet of the old stock gan to shoot again,
Or it men's follies mote be forced to feign,
And roll with rest in rhymes of ribaldry,
Or as it sprung, it wither must again:
Tom Piper makes us better melody.

14
*Piers:*   O peerless poesie, where is then thy place,
If nor in prince's palace thou do sit
(And yet is prince's palace thee most fit)
Ne breast of baser birth doth thee embrace?
Then make thee wings of thine aspiring wit,
And, whence thou cam'st, fly back to heaven
apace.

.5   **eft** afterwards   11.3   **liggen** lie   .6   **aye** always   12.2
**brought a-bed of** brought to bed by   .3 **vaunting** glorifying
**pease** pea, i.e., something so small as to be valueless   .4 **put in
press** crowd, exercise   13.3 **or** either   **mote** must   **feign** imi-
tate, depict   .6 **Tom Piper** a simple rustic   14.2 **nor . . . ne**
neither . . . nor

15

Cuddie:   Ah Percy, it is all too weak and wan
          So high to soar, and make so large a flight;
          Her piecéd pinions been not so in plight;
          For Colin fits such famous flight to scan:
          He, were he not with love so ill bedight,
          Would mount as high and sing as sweet as swan.

16

Piers:    Ah, fon; for love does teach him climb so high,
          And lifts him up out of the loathesome mire:
          Such immortal mirror as he doth admire
          Would raise one's mind above the starry sky
          And cause a caitiff courage to aspire:
          For lofty love doth loathe a lowly eye.

17

Cuddie:   All otherwise the state of poet stands,
          For lordly love is such a tyrant fell
          That where he rules, all power he doth expel;
          The vaunted verse a vacant head demands,
          Ne wont with crabbéd care the Muses dwell.
          Unwisely weaves, that takes two webs in hand.

18

          Whoever casts to compass weighty prize,
          And thinks to throw out thundering words of
              threat,
          Let pour in lavish cups and thrifty bits of meat,
          For Bacchus' fruit is friend to Phoebus wise;
          And when with wine the brain begins to sweat,
          The numbers flow as fast as spring doth rise.

---

15.3 **piecéd** patched   **so in plight** in such good condition   .4
**for Colin . . . fits** it is suitable for Colin (pseudonym for Spenser)   **scan** mount to   .5 **ill bedight** disarrayed   16.1 **fon** fool
.5 **caitiff courage** low, or mean, mind or heart   17.2 **fell** terrible   18.3 **thrifty** substantial

19
Thou kenst not, Percy, how the rhyme should
   rage.
O if my temples were distained with wine,
And girt in garlands of wild ivy twine,
How I could rear the Muse on stately stage,
And teach her tread aloft in buskin fine,
With quaint Bellona in her equipage!

20
But ah, my courage cools ere it be warm;
For-thy, content us in this humble shade,
Where no such troublous tides han us assayed;
Here we our slender pipes may safely charm.
Piers:   And when my gates shall han their bellies laid,
Cuddie shall have a kid to store his farm.

Cuddie's Emblem:

*Agitante calescimus illo,* etc.

19.1 **kenst** know[est]   .2 **distained** stained   .5 **buskin** classical
footgear for an actor in tragedy   .6 **quaint** strange, remarkable
**Bellona** goddess of war   20.4 **charm** tune, play   .5 **gates** goats
.5 **han . . . laid** be delivered   **Emblem** the emblem, or motto,
is a quotation from Ovid's *Fasti*: "There is a god in us, and
through his influence we are warmed by inspiration." The refer-
ence here is, obviously, to the divine nature of poetic inspiration

# from Amoretti

## 8

More than most fair, full of the living fire
Kindled above unto the Maker near:
No eyes, but joys, in which all powers conspire
That to the world naught else be counted dear.
Through your bright beams doth not the blinded guest    5
Shoot out his darts to base affections wound;
But angels come, to lead frail minds to rest
In chaste desires, on heavenly beauty bound.
You frame my thoughts and fashion me within;
You stop my tongue, and teach my heart to speak;    10
You calm the storm that passion did begin,
Strong through your cause, but by your virtue weak.
Dark is the world where your light shinéd never;
Well is he born that may behold you ever.

## 28

The laurel leaf which you this day do wear
Gives me great hope of your relenting mind:
For, since it is the badge which I do bear,
Ye, bearing it, do seem to me inclined.

8.5 **blinded guest** Cupid   28.3 **badge** laurel was associated
with poets.

7

The power thereof, which oft in me I find,                    5
Let it likewise your gentle breast inspire
With sweet infusion, and put you in mind
Of that proud maid whom now those leaves attire:
Proud Daphne, scorning Phoebus' lovely fire,
On the Thessalian shore from him did flee,              10
For which the gods in their revengeful ire
Did her transform into a laurel tree.
Then fly no more, fair love, from Phoebus' chase,
But in your breast his leaf and love embrace.

# 30

My love is like to ice, and I to fire;
How comes it, then, that this her cold so great
Is not dissolved through my so hot desire,
But harder grows the more I her entreat?
Or how comes it that my exceeding heat                    5
Is not delayed by her heart frozen cold,
But that I burn much more in boiling sweat,
And feel my flames augmented manifold?
What more miraculous thing may be told,
That fire, which all things melts, should harden ice:     10
And ice, which is congealed with senseless cold,
Should kindle fire, by wonderful device?
Such is the power of love in gentle mind
That it can alter all the course of kind.

.9 **lovely fire** loving ardor, but also fieriness, because Phoebus is
the sun god (and the god of poets; see last line)   30.7 **boiling**
the lady's name was Boyle   .11 **senseless** insensible   .14 **kind**
nature

# 44

When those renowméd noble peers of Greece
Through stubborn pride amongst themselves did jar,
Forgetful of the famous golden fleece,
Then Orpheus with his harp their strife did bar;
But this continual cruel civil war,                              5
The which myself against myself do make,
Whilst my weak powers of passions warreid are,
No skill can stint, nor reason can aslake.
But when in hand my tuneless harp I take,
Then do I more augment my foes' despite,          10
And grief renew, and passions do awake
To battle, fresh against myself to fight—
'Mongst whom the more I seek to settle peace,
The more I find their malice to increase.

# 68

Most glorious Lord of life, that on this day
Didst make Thy triumph over death and sin,
And having harrowed hell didst bring away
Captivity thence captive, us to win:
This joyous day, dear Lord, with joy begin,          5
And grant that we for whom Thou diddest die,
Being with Thy dear blood clean washed from sin,
May live forever in felicity;
And that, Thy love we weighing worthily,
May likewise love Thee for the same again,          10

44.1 **renowméd** renowned **peers of Greece** the Argonauts
.7 **warreid** assailed  .10 **despite** spite  68.1 **this day** Easter

And for Thy sake, that all like dear didst buy,
With love may one another entertain.
So let us love, dear love, like as we ought;
Love is the lesson which the Lord us taught.

# 70

Fresh Spring, the herald of love's mighty king,
In whose coat-armor richly are displayed
All sorts of flowers the which on earth do spring,
In goodly colors gloriously arrayed:
Go to my love, where she is careless laid,                    5
Yet in her winter's bower, not well awake;
Tell her the joyous time will not be stayed
Unless she do him by the forelock take.
Bid her therefore herself soon ready make
To wait on Love amongst his lovely crew,                      10
Where everyone that misseth then her make
Shall be by him amerced with penance due.
Make haste therefore, sweet love, whilst it is prime,
For none can call again the passéd time.

# 75

One day I wrote her name upon the strand,
But came the waves and washéd it away;
Again I wrote it with a second hand,
But came the tide, and made my pains his prey.

.11 **like dear** with equal expense (suffering)   .12 **entertain**
maintain, receive   70.2 **coat-armor** tunic with coat of arms
.5 **careless** unconcerned   .11 **make** mate   .12 **amerced** pun-
ished   .13 **prime** morning or spring (morning of the year)

Vain man, said she, that dost in vain assay 5
A mortal thing so to immortalize;
For I myself shall like to this decay,
And eke my name be wipéd out likewise.
Not so (quoth I); let baser things devise
To die in dust, but you shall live by fame: 10
My verse your virtues rare shall eternize,
And in the heavens write your glorious name,
Where, whenas Death shall all the world subdue,
Our love shall live, and later life renew.

75.8 **eke** also

# Epithalamion

1]  Ye learnéd sisters, which have oftentimes
    Been to me aiding, others to adorn,
    Whom ye thought worthy of your graceful rhymes,
    That even the greatest did not greatly scorn
    To hear their names sung in your simple lays,        5
    But joyéd in their praise;
    And when ye list your own mishaps to mourn,
    Which death or love or fortune's wreck did raise,
    Your string could soon to sadder tenor turn,
    And teach the woods and waters to lament        10
    Your doleful dreariment:
    Now lay those sorrowful complaints aside,
    And having all your heads with garland crowned,
    Help me mine own love's praises to resound,
    Ne let the same of any be envied:        15
    So Orpheus did for his own bride,
    So I unto myself alone will sing;
    The woods shall to me answer and my echo ring.

According to the theory explained in A. Kent Hieatt, *Short Time's Endless Monument* (New York, 1960), the *Epithalamion* reinforces the idea of marriage as the beginning of a new cycle of human life by embodying in arithmetical form the renewal of the apparent cycle of the sun through the 24 hours (24 stanzas of the day) and the 365 days (365 long lines—lines of 5 or 6 feet, contrasting with the short lines of 3 feet) of the year. The stanzas of daylight (16¼) with positive refrains (e.g., 1.18) and the stanzas of darkness (7¾) with negative refrains (e.g., 17.17) correspond in number to the hours of day and night on the longest day of the year, the day on which the poem takes place (15.11), at least in the latitude of southern Ireland where Spenser married Elizabeth Boyle. The idea of the individual's participation in a cyclical cosmic dance where decay and death are mitigated in the eternal recurrence of all—the eternal pattern of the universe—appears in *The Faerie Queene*, III, vi, 29–48  **1.1 sisters** the Muses  **.15 Ne** nor

2]  Early, before the world's light-giving lamp
   His golden beam upon the hills doth spread,
   Having dispersed the night's uncheerful damp,
   Do ye awake, and with fresh lustihead
   Go to the bower of my belovéd love,                   5
   My truest turtle dove:
   Bid her awake, for Hymen is awake,
   And long since ready forth his masque to move,
   With his bright tead that flames with many a flake,
   And many a bachelor to wait on him,             10
   In their fresh garments trim.
   Bid her awake, therefore, and soon her dight,
   For lo the wishéd day is come at last
   That shall for all the pains and sorrows past
   Pay to her usury of long delight:                15
   And whilst she doth her dight,
   Do ye to her of joy and solace sing,
   That all the woods may answer, and your echo ring.

3]  Bring with you all the nymphs that you can hear,
   Both of the rivers and the forests green,
   And of the sea that neighbors to her near,
   All with gay garlands goodly well beseen.
   And let them also with them bring in hand         5
   Another gay garland
   For my fair love, of lilies and of roses,
   Bound true-love wise with a blue silk ribband.
   And let them make great store of bridal posies,
   And let them eke bring store of other flowers     10
   To deck the bridal bowers.
   And let the ground whereas her foot shall tread,
   For fear the stones her tender foot should wrong,
   Be strewed with fragrant flowers all along,
   And diapred like the discolored mead.             15
   Which done, do at her chamber door await,
   For she will waken straight;
   The whiles do ye this song unto her sing,
   The woods shall to you answer, and your echo ring.

2.4 **lustihead** (-hood) lustiness  .8 **masque** pageant  .9 **tead**
torch  **flake** flash  3.15 **diapred** patterned  **discolored** multi-
colored

4] Ye nymphs of Mulla, which with careful heed
The silver scaly trouts do tend full well,
And greedy pikes which use thereon to feed
(Those trouts and pikes all others do excel),
And ye likewise which keep the rushy lake          5
Where none do fishes take,
Bind up the locks the which hang scattered light,
And in his waters, which your mirror make,
Behold your faces as the crystal bright,
That when you come whereas my love doth lie        10
No blemish she may spy.
And eke ye lightfoot maids which keep the deer
That on the hoary mountains use to tower,
And the wild wolves, which seek them to devour,
With your steel darts do chase from coming near,   15
Be also present here,
To help to deck her and to help to sing,
That all the woods may answer, and your echo ring.

5] Wake now, my love, awake; for it is time:
The rosy morn long since left Tithon's bed,
All ready to her silver coach to climb,
And Phoebus gins to show his glorious head.
Hark how the cheerful birds do chant their lays    5
And carol of love's praise.
The merry lark her matins sings aloft,
The thrush replies, the mavis descant plays,
The ouzel shrills, the ruddock warbles soft,
So goodly all agree with sweet consent,            10
To this day's merriment.
Ah my dear love, why do ye sleep thus long,
When meeter were that ye should now awake
T'await the coming of your joyous make,
And hearken to the birds' love-learnéd song,       15
The dewy leaves among.
For they of joy and pleasance to you sing,
That all the woods them answer, and their echo ring.

4.1 **Mulla** a river near the scene of the marriage   .13 **tower**
fly up   5.10 **consent** harmony

6] My love is now awake out of her dream,
   And her fair eyes, like stars that dimméd were
   With darksome cloud, now show their goodly beams,
   More bright than Hesperus his head doth rear.
   Come now, ye damsels, daughters of delight,       5
   Help quickly her to dight,
   But first come ye, fair Hours, which were begot
   In Jove's sweet paradise, of Day and Night,
   Which do the seasons of the year allot,
   And all that ever in this world is fair       10
   Do make and still repair.
   And ye three handmaids of the Cyprian queen,
   The which do still adorn her beauty's pride,
   Help to adorn my beautifullest bride:
   And as ye her array, still throw between       15
   Some graces to be seen,
   And as ye use to Venus, to her sing,
   The whiles the woods shall answer, and your echo ring.

7] Now is my love all ready forth to come;
   Let all the virgins therefore well await,
   And ye fresh boys that tend upon her groom,
   Prepare yourselves, for he is coming straight.
   Set all your things in seemly good array       5
   Fit for so joyful day,
   The joyful'st day that ever sun did see.
   Fair sun, show forth thy favorable ray,
   And let thy lifeful heat not fervent be,
   For fear of burning her sunshiny face,       10
   Her beauty to disgrace.
   O fairest Phoebus, father of the Muse,
   If ever I did honor thee aright,
   Or sing the thing that mote thy mind delight,
   Do not thy servant's simple boon refuse,       15
   But let this day, let this one day be mine:
   Let all the rest be thine.

6.12 **handmaids** the Graces **Cyprian queen** Venus .13 **still**
continually .15 **between** at intervals of time 7.4 **straight**
straightaway .14 **mote** might

Then I thy sovereign praises loud will sing,
That all the woods shall answer, and their echo ring.

8]   Hark how the minstrels gin to shrill aloud
Their merry music that resounds from far,
The pipe, the tabor, and the trembling crowd,
That well agree withouten breach or jar.
But most of all the damsels do delight                          5
When they their timbrels smite,
And thereunto do dance and carol sweet,
That all the senses they do ravish quite,
The whiles the boys run up and down the street,
Crying aloud with strong confuséd noise                       10
As if it were one voice.
*Hymen io Hymen, Hymen,* they do shout,
That even to the heavens their shouting shrill
Doth reach, and all the firmament doth fill,
To which the people standing all about,                       15
As in approvance, do thereto applaud
And loud advance her laud,
And evermore they *Hymen Hymen* sing,
That all the woods them answer, and their echo ring.

9]   Lo where she comes along with portly pace,
Like Phoebe from her chamber of the east,
Arising forth to run her mighty race,
Clad all in white, that seems a virgin best.
So well it her beseems that ye would ween                     5
Some angel she had been.
Her long, loose, yellow locks like golden wire,
Sprinkled with pearl, and pearling flowers a-tween,
Do like a golden mantle her attire,
And being crownéd with a garland green,                       10
Seem like some maiden queen.
Her modest eyes, abashéd to behold
So many gazers as on her do stare,
Upon the lowly ground affixéd are,
Ne dare lift up her countenance too bold,                     15
But blush to hear her praises sung so loud,

8.3 **crowd** viol   .12 **Hymen** . . . traditional invocation of the
god of marriage   9.2 **Phoebe** the moon   .4 **seems** suits

So far from being proud.
Nath'less do ye still loud her praises sing,
That all the woods may answer, and your echo ring.

10]  Tell me, ye merchants' daughters, did ye see
So fair a creature in your town before,
So sweet, so lovely, and so mild as she,
Adorned with beauty's grace and virtue's store,
Her goodly eyes like sapphires shining bright,        5
Her forehead ivory white,
Her cheeks like apples which the sun hath rudded,
Her lips like cherries charming men to bite,
Her breast like to a bowl of cream uncrudded,
Her paps like lilies budded,        10
Her snowy neck like to a marble tower,
And all her body like a palace fair,
Ascending up with many a stately stair
To honor's seat and chastity's sweet bower?
Why stand ye still, ye virgins, in amaze,        15
Upon her so to gaze,
Whiles ye forget your former lay to sing,
To which the woods did answer, and your echo ring?

11]  But if ye saw that which no eyes can see,
The inward beauty of her lively spright,
Garnished with heavenly gifts of high degree,
Much more then would ye wonder at that sight,
And stand astonished like to those which read        5
Medusa's mazeful head.
There dwells sweet love and constant chastity,
Unspotted faith and comely womanhead,
Regard of honor and mild majesty;
There virtue reigns as queen in royal throne,        10
And giveth laws alone,
The which the base affections do obey,
And yield their services unto her will,
Ne thought of thing uncomely ever may
Thereto approach to tempt her mind to ill.        15
Had ye once seen these her celestial treasures

10.9 **uncrudded** uncurdled  11.2 **spright** spirit  .5 **read** saw
.6 **mazeful** amazing; also, wandering in snaky locks

And unrevealéd pleasures,
Then would ye wonder and her praises sing,
That all the woods should answer, and your echo ring.

12] Open the temple gates unto my love,
Open them wide that she may enter in,
And all the posts adorn as doth behoove,
And all the pillars deck with garlands trim,
For to receive this saint with honor due                    5
That cometh in to you.
With trembling steps and humble reverence
She cometh in, before th'Almighty's view;
Of her ye virgins learn obedience:
When so ye come into those holy places,                    10
To humble your proud faces:
Bring her up to th'high altar, that she may
The sacred ceremonies there partake,
The which do endless matrimony make,
And let the roaring organs loudly play                      15
The praises of the Lord in lively notes,
The whiles with hollow throats
The choristers the joyous anthem sing,
That all the woods may answer, and their echo ring.

13] Behold, whiles she before the altar stands
Hearing the holy priest that to her speaks
And blesseth her with his two happy hands,
How the red roses flush up in her cheeks,
And the pure snow with goodly vermeil stain,               5
Like crimson dyed in grain,
That even th' angels, which continually
About the sacred altar do remain,
Forget their service and about her fly,
Oft peeping in her face, that seems more fair              10
The more they on it stare.
But her sad eyes, still fastened on the ground,
Are governéd with goodly modesty
That suffers not one look to glance awry
Which may let in a little thought unsound.                 15
Why blush ye, love, to give to me your hand,

13.3 **happy** promising felicity   .12 **sad** sober

The pledge of all our band?
Sing ye, sweet angels, *Alleluia* sing,
That all the woods may answer, and your echo ring.


14]  Now all is done; bring home the bride again,
Bring home the triumph of our victory,
Bring home with you the glory of her gain,
With joyance bring her and with jollity.
Never had man more joyful day than this                          5
Whom heaven would heap with bliss.
Make feast therefore now all this live-long day;
This day forever to me holy is;
Pour out the wine without restraint or stay,
Pour not by cups, but by the belly-ful,                         10
Pour out to all that will,
And sprinkle all the posts and walls with wine,
That they may sweat, and drunken be withal.
Crown ye god Bacchus with a coronal,
And Hymen also crown with wreaths of vine,                      15
And let the Graces dance unto the rest,
For they can do it best:
The whiles the maidens do their carol sing,
To which the woods shall answer, and their echo ring.


15]  Ring ye the bells, ye young men of the town,
And leave your wonted labors for this day:
This day is holy; do ye write it down,
That ye forever it remember may.
This day the sun is in his chiefest height,                     5
With Barnaby the bright,
From whence declining daily by degrees,
He somewhat loseth of his heat and light,
When once the Crab behind his back he sees.
But for this time it ill ordainéd was                           10
To choose the longest day in all the year,
And shortest night, when longest fitter were:


.17 **band** tie, bond    15.6 **Barnaby** St. Barnabas' Day then fell
on the longest day in the year, the summer solstice. After the
solstice, the sun declines along the Zodiac about one degree per
day and passes the sign of the Crab, Cancer

Yet never day so long but late would pass.
Ring ye the bells, to make it wear away,
And bonfires make all day,                              15
And dance about them, and about them sing:
That all the woods may answer, and your echo ring.

16]  Ah, when will this long, weary day have end,
And lend me leave to come unto my love?
How slowly do the hours their numbers spend!
How slowly does sad Time his feathers move!
Haste thee, O fairest planet, to thy home              5
Within the western foam:
Thy tired steeds long since have need of rest.
Long though it be, at last I see it gloam,
And the bright evening star with golden crest
Appear out of the east.                                10
Fair child of beauty, glorious lamp of love,
That all the host of heaven in ranks dost lead
And guidest lovers through the nightés dread,
How cheerfully thou lookest from above
And seemst to laugh atween thy twinkling light,        15
As joying in the sight
Of these glad many which for joy do sing,
That all the woods them answer, and their echo ring.

17]  Now cease, ye damsels, your delights forepast;
Enough is it, that all the day was yours;
Now day is done, and night is nighing fast:
Now bring the bride into the bridal bowers.
Now night is come, now soon her disarray,              5
And in her bed her lay;
Lay her in lilies and in violets,
And silken curtains over her display,
And odored sheets, and Arras coverlets.
Behold how goodly my fair love does lie                10
In proud humility;
Like unto Maia, whenas Jove her took
In Tempe, lying on the flowry grass,
'Twixt sleep and wake, after she weary was
With bathing in the Acidalian brook.                   15

16.5 **planet**  the sun

Now it is night, ye damsels may be gone
And leave my love alone,
And leave likewise your former lay to sing:
The woods no more shall answer, nor your echo ring.

18]  Now welcome night, thou night so long expected
That long days' labor dost at last defray,
And all my cares, which cruel love collected,
Hast summed in one, and cancelléd for aye:
Spread thy broad wing over my love and me     5
That no man may us see,
And in thy sable mantle us enwrap,
From fear of peril and foul horror free.
Let no false treason seek us to entrap,
Nor any dread disquiet once annoy     10
The safety of our joy:
But let the night be calm and quietsome,
Without tempestuous storms or sad affray,
Like as when Jove with fair Alcmena lay,
When he begot the great Tirynthian groom:     15
Or like as when he with thyself did lie,
And begot Majesty.
And let the maids and young men cease to sing:
Ne let the woods them answer, nor their echo ring.

19]  Let no lamenting cries nor doleful tears
Be heard all night within nor yet without:
Ne let false whispers, breeding hidden fears,
Break gentle sleep with misconceivéd doubt.
Let no deluding dreams nor dreadful sights     5
Make sudden sad affrights;
Ne let house fires, nor lightning's helpless harms,
Ne let the Puck, nor other evil sprites,
Ne let mischievous witches with their charms,
Ne let hobgoblins, names whose sense we see not,     10
Fray us with things that be not.
Let not the screech owl nor the stork be heard,
Nor the night raven that still deadly yells,
Nor damnéd ghosts called up with mighty spells,

18.15 **Tirynthian groom** Hercules  .16 **thyself** Night  19.7
**helpless** irremediable  .11 **fray** frighten

Nor grisly vultures make us once afeared;                    15
Ne let th'unpleasant choir of frogs still croaking
Make us to wish their choking.
Let none of these their dreary accents sing;
Ne let the woods them answer, nor their echo ring.

20] But let still silence true night watches keep,
That sacred peace may in assurance reign,
And timely sleep, when it is time to sleep,
May pour his limbs forth on your pleasant plain,
The whiles an hundred little wingéd loves,         5
Like divers feathered doves,
Shall fly and flutter round about your bed,
And in the secret dark, that none reproves,
Their pretty stealths shall work, and snares shall spread
To filch away sweet snatches of delight,           10
Concealed through covert night.
Ye sons of Venus, play your sports at will,
For greedy Pleasure, careless of your toys,
Thinks more upon her paradise of joys
Than what ye do, albeit good or ill.               15
All night therefore attend your merry play,
For it will soon be day:
Now none doth hinder you that say or sing,
Ne will the woods now answer, nor your echo ring.

21] Who is the same which at my window peeps?
Or whose is that fair face that shines so bright?
Is it not Cynthia, she that never sleeps,
But walks about high heaven all the night?
O fairest goddess, do thou not envy               5
My love with me to spy:
For thou likewise didst love, though now unthought,
And for a fleece of wool, which privily
The Latmian shepherd once unto thee brought,
His pleasures with thee wrought.                   10
Therefore to us be favorable now;
And sith of women's labors thou hast charge,
And generation goodly dost enlarge,
Incline thy will t'effect our wishful vow,

20.5 **loves** cupids   21.9 **Latmian shepherd** Endymion   .12
**labors** in the sense of childbirth

And the chaste womb inform with timely seed                    15
That may our comfort breed:
Till which we cease our hopeful hap to sing,
Ne let the woods us answer, nor our echo ring.

22]   And thou, great Juno, which with awful might
The laws of wedlock still dost patronize,
And the religion of the faith first plight
With sacred rites hast taught to solemnize—
And eke for comfort often calléd art                          5
Of women in their smart—
Eternally bind thou this lovely band,
And all thy blessings unto us impart.
And thou, glad Genius, in whose gentle hand
The bridal bower and genial bed remain,                       10
Without blemish or stain,
And the sweet pleasures of their love's delight
With secret aid dost succor and supply
Till they bring forth the fruitful progeny,
Send us the timely fruit of this same night.                  15
And thou, fair Hebe, and thou, Hymen free,
Grant that it may so be.
Till which we cease your further praise to sing,
Ne any woods shall answer, nor your echo ring.

23]   And ye high heavens, the temple of the gods,
In which a thousand torches flaming bright
Do burn, that to us wretched earthly clods
In dreadful darkness lend desiréd light,
And all ye powers which in the same remain,                   5
More than we men can feign,
Pour out your blessings on us plenteously,
And happy influence upon us rain,
That we may raise a large posterity,
Which from the earth, which they may long possess             10
With lasting happiness,
Up to your haughty palaces may mount,
And for the guerdon of their glorious merit,
May heavenly tabernacles there inherit,
Of blesséd saints for to increase the count.                  15

22.3 **religion** scrupulousness   .9 **Genius** spirit of natural generation   23.6 **feign** describe, imagine

So let us rest, sweet love, in hope of this,
And cease till then our timely joys to sing;
The woods no more us answer, nor our echo ring.

24]  Song made in lieu of many ornaments,
With which my love should duly have been decked,
Which cutting off through hasty accidents,
Ye would not stay your due time to expect,
But promised both to recompense,                                        5
Be unto her a goodly ornament,
And for short time an endless monument.

24.1 **Song . . . ornaments**  according to the theory mentioned in
the note at the beginning of the poem, this last short stanza covers
the discrepancy between the apparent daily motion of the sun and
that of the fixed stars: when the fixed stars have completed their
orbit, moving from east to west, the sun has gone only 359° in
this direction (the last line of the previous stanza is, accordingly,
the 359th long line of the poem). The sun thus does not "stay"
to await his "due time"; instead, he embarks on his other journey,
from west to east, which carries him back almost exactly one de-
gree daily, as implied above, so that in 365 days he has completed
his opposite circle and made the year. The cycle of the year, with
its seasonal support of our life, is the "recompense" for the failure
of the sun to come at his "due time." The last stanza is a "re-
compense" in the same way: it brings the total of long lines to 365

# from The Faerie Queene

## Book I

### Canto ii

*Book I tells of the progress of the Knight of Holiness,
called the Redcross Knight or Saint George (patron saint
of England), whose mission is to come to the aid of the
lady Una (oneness, truth). But the enchanter Archimago
misleads him into believing Una has been unchaste. Red-
cross deserts Una and falls into the toils of the witch
Duessa (doubleness, therefore falseness), who represents
herself as Fidessa (faithfulness); and for a while he is in
great danger. [Eds.]*

7]  Now when the rosy-fingered Morning fair,
   Weary of aged Tithonus' saffron bed,
   Had spread her purple robe through dewy air,
   And the high hills Titan discoveréd,
   The royal virgin shook off drowsyhead,
   And rising forth out of her baser bower,
   Looked for her knight, who far away was fled,
   And for her dwarf, that wont to wait each hour;
   Then gan she wail and weep, to see that woeful stour.

8]  And after him she rode with so much speed
   As her slow beast could make, but all in vain:
   For him so far had borne his light-foot steed,

7.4 **Titan** the sun   .5 **royal virgin** Una   **-head** -hood
.9 **stour** misfortune

Prickéd with wrath and fiery fierce disdain,
That him to follow was but fruitless pain;
Yet she her weary limbs would never rest,
But every hill and dale, each wood and plain,
Did search, sore grievéd in her gentle breast,
He so ungently left her, whom she lovéd best.

9] But subtle Archimago, when his guests
　He saw divided into double parts,
　And Una wandering in woods and forests—
　Th'end of his drift—he praised his devilish arts
　That had such might over true meaning hearts;
　Yet rests not so, but other means doth make,
　How he may work unto her further smarts:
　For her he hated as the hissing snake,
　And in her many troubles did most pleasure take.

10] He then devised himself how to disguise;
　For by his mighty science he could take
　As many forms and shapes in seeming wise
　As ever Proteus to himself could make:
　Sometime a fowl, sometime a fish in lake,
　Now like a fox, now like a dragon fell—
　That of himself he oft for fear would quake,
　And oft would fly away. O who can tell
　The hidden power of herbs, and might of magic spell?

11] But now seemed best, the person to put on
　Of that good knight, his late beguiléd guest;
　In mighty arms he was yclad anon,
　And silver shield: upon his coward breast
　A bloody cross, and on his craven crest
　A bunch of hairs discolored diversly:
　Full jolly knight he seemed, and well addressed,
　And when he sat upon his courser free,
　Saint George himself ye would have deeméd him to be.

12] But he, the knight whose semblance he did bear—
　The true Saint George—was wandered far away,

8.8 **gentle** noble　9.4 **Th'end . . . drift** which was his purpose
11.6 **discolored** multicolored

Still flying from his thoughts and jealous fear;
Will was his guide, and grief led him astray.
At last him chanced to meet upon the way
A faithless Saracen all armed to point,
In whose great shield was writ with letters gay
Sans Foy: full large of limb and every joint
He was, and caréd not for God or man a point.

13] He had a fair companion of his way,
A goodly lady clad in scarlet red,
Purfled with gold and pearl of rich assay,
And like a Persian mitre on her head
She wore, with crowns and ouches garnishéd,
The which her lavish lovers to her gave;
Her wanton palfrey all was overspread
With tinsel trappings, woven like a wave,
Whose bridle rung with golden bells and bosses brave.

14] With fair disport and courting dalliance
She entertained her lover all the way:
But when she saw the knight his spear advance,
She soon left off her mirth and wanton play,
And bad her knight address him to the fray:
His foe was nigh at hand. He, pricked with pride
And hope to win his lady's heart that day,
Forth spurréd fast: adown his courser's side
The red blood trickling stained the way as he did ride.

15] The knight of the Redcross, when him he spied,
Spurring so hot with rage dispiteous,
Gan fairly couch his spear, and towards ride:
Soon meet they both, both fell and furious,
That daunted with their forces hideous,
Their steeds do stagger and amazéd stand,
And eke themselves too rudely rigorous,
Astonied with the stroke of their own hand,
Do back rebut, and each to other yieldeth land.

12.8 **Sans foy** without faith  .9 **point** speck  13.4 **mitre** these
details of dress suggest the Whore of Babylon (Revelation
17:3–5), often equated with the Roman Catholic Church by
Protestants of Spenser's time  .5 **ouches** ornaments

16] As when two rams, stirred with ambitious pride,
Fight for the rule of the rich fleecéd flock,
Their hornéd fronts so fierce on either side
Do meet, that with the terror of the shock
Astonied both, stand senseless as a block,
Forgetful of the hanging victory:
So stood these twain, unmovéd as a rock,
Both staring fierce, and holding idlely
The broken relics of their former cruelty.


17] The Saracen, sore daunted with the buff,
Snatcheth his sword, and fiercely to him flies,
Who well it wards, and quitteth cuff with cuff:
Each other's equal puissance envies,
And through their iron sides with cruel spies
Does seek to pierce: repining courage yields
No foot to foe. The flashing fire flies
As from a forge out of their burning shields,
And streams of purple blood new dyes the verdant fields.


18] Curse on that Cross (quoth then the Saracen)
That keeps thy body from the bitter fit;
Dead long ago I wot thou haddest been,
Had not that charm from thee forwarnéd it:
But yet I warn thee now assuréd sit,
And hide thy head.—Therewith upon his crest
With rigor so outrageous he smit
That a large share it hewed out of the rest,
And glancing down his shield, from blame him fairly
    blessed.


19] Who thereat wondrous wroth, the sleeping spark
Of native virtue gan eftsoons revive,
And at his haughty helmet making mark,
So hugely stroke that it the steel did rive,
And cleft his head. He tumbling down alive,
With bloody mouth his mother earth did kiss,


17.3 **quitteth** repays   .5 **spies** glances   .6 **repining** angry
18.2 **fit** i.e., death   .9 **from . . . blessed** failed to harm him

Greeting his grave: his grudging ghost did strive
With the frail flesh; at last it flitted is,
Whither the souls do fly of men that live amiss.

20] The lady, when she saw her champion fall
Like the old ruins of a broken tower,
Stayed not to wail his woeful funeral;
But from him fled away with all her power,
Who after her as hastily gan scour,
Bidding the dwarf with him to bring away
The Saracen's shield, sign of the conqueror.
Her soon he overtook, and bad to stay,
For present cause was none of dread her to dismay.

21] She turning back with rueful countenance,
Cried: Mercy, mercy, Sir, vouchsafe to show
On silly dame, subject to hard mischance,
And to your mighty will.—Her humblesse low,
In so rich weeds and seeming glorious show,
Did much enmove his stout heroic heart,
And said: Dear dame, your sudden overthrow
Much rueth me; but now put fear apart,
And tell both who ye be, and who that took your part.

22] Melting in tears, then gan she thus lament:
The wretched woman, whom unhappy hour
Hath now made thrall to your commandement,
Before that angry heavens list to lower,
And Fortune false betrayed me to your power,
Was (O what now availeth that I was!)
Born the sole daughter of an Emperor,
He that the wide West under his rule has,
And high hath set his throne, where Tiberis doth pass.

23] He, in the first flower of my freshest age,
Betrothéd me unto the only heir
Of a most mighty king, most rich and sage;
Was never Prince so faithful and so fair,

20.9 **For . . . dismay** there was no cause of dread present to
dismay her  21.8 **rueth me** causes me sorrow  22.9 **Tiberis** the
Tiber river; a key to the allegory of stanzas 22–24, and later

Was never Prince so meek and debonair;
But ere my hopéd day of spousal shone,
My dearest Lord fell from high honor's stair
Into the hands of his accursed fone,
And cruelly was slain; that shall I ever moan.

24] His blesséd body spoiled of lively breath,
Was afterward—I know not how—conveyed
And from me hid: of whose most innocent death
When tidings came to me, unhappy maid,
O how great sorrow my sad soul assayed.
Then forth I went, his woeful corse to find,
And many years throughout the world I strayed,
A virgin widow, whose deep wounded mind
With love long time did languish as the stricken hind.

25] At last it chancéd this proud Saracen
To meet me wandering, who perforce me led
With him away, but yet could never win
The fort that ladies hold in sovereign dread.
There lies he now with foul dishonor dead,
Who while he lived was calléd proud Sans foy,
The eldest of three brethren, all three bred
Of one bad sire, whose youngest is Sans joy,
And 'twixt them both was born the bloody bold Sans loy.

26] In this sad plight, friendless, unfortunate,
Now miserable, I Fidessa dwell,
Craving of you, in pity of my state,
To do none ill, if please ye not do well.
—He in great passion all this while did dwell,
More busying his quick eyes, her face to view,
Than his dull ears, to hear what she did tell;
And said: Fair lady, heart of flint would rue
The undeservéd woes and sorrows which ye shew.

27] Henceforth in safe assurance may ye rest,
Having both found a new friend you to aid,
And lost an old foe, that did you molest:
Better new friend than an old foe is said.

23.8 **fone** foes  25.9 **loy** loyalty

With change of cheer the seeming simple maid
Let fall her eyes, as shamefast, to the earth,
And yielding soft, in that she nought gainsaid;
So forth they rode, he feigning seemly mirth,
And she coy looks: so dainty they say maketh dearth.

28]  Long time they thus together travelléd,
Till weary of their way they came at last
Where grew two goodly trees, that fair did spread
Their arms abroad, with gray moss overcast,
And their green leaves trembling with every blast
Made a calm shadow far in compass round:
The fearful shepherd, often there aghast,
Under them never sat, ne wont there sound
His merry oaten pipe, but shunned th'unlucky ground.

29]  But this good knight, soon as he them can spy,
For the cool shade him thither hast'ly got:
For golden Phoebus, now ymounted high,
From fiery wheels of his fair chariot
Hurléd his beam so scorching cruel hot
That living creature mote it not abide;
And his new lady it enduréd not.
There they alight, in hope themselves to hide
From the fierce heat, and rest their weary limbs a tide.

30]  Fair seemly pleasance each to other makes,
With goodly purposes there as they sit:
And in his falséd fancy he her takes
To be the fairest wight that livéd yet;
Which to express, he bends his gentle wit,
And thinking of those branches green to frame
A garland for her dainty forehead fit,
He plucked a bough, out of whose rift there came
Small drops of gory blood that trickled down the same.

31]  Therewith a piteous yelling voice was heard,
Crying: O spare with guilty hands to tear
My tender sides in this rough rind embarred,

27.9 **dainty . . . dearth** lack (of, e.g., a companion) makes the
scarce item desirable   28.8 **ne** nor   30.3 **falséd** deceived   31.3
**embarred** imprisoned

But fly, ah fly far hence away, for fear
Lest to you hap, that happened to me here,
And to this wretched lady, my dear love—
O too dear love: love bought with death too dear.
—Aston'd he stood, and up his hair did hove,
And with that sudden horror could no member move.

32]   At last whenas the dreadful passión
Was overpassed, and manhood well awake,
Yet musing at the strange occasión,
And doubting much his sense, he thus bespake:
What voice of damnéd ghost from Limbo lake,
Or guileful sprite wandering in empty air—
Both which frail men do oftentimes mistake—
Sends to my doubtful ears these speeches rare,
And rueful plaints, me bidding guiltless blood to spare?

33]   Then groaning deep: Nor damnéd ghost (quoth he)
Nor guileful sprite to thee these words doth speak,
But once a man, Fradubio, now a tree:
Wretched man, wretched tree!—whose nature weak,
A cruel witch, her cursed will to wreak,
Hath thus transformed, and placed in open plains,
Where Boreas doth blow full bitter bleak,
And scorching sun does dry my secret veins:
For though a tree I seem, yet cold and heat me pains.

34]   Say on, Fradubio, then, or man or tree—
Quoth then the knight—by whose mischievous arts
Art thou misshapéd thus, as now I see?
He oft finds med'cine, who his grief imparts;
But double griefs afflict concealing hearts,
As raging flames who striveth to suppress.
The author then, (said he) of all my smarts,
Is one Duessa, a false sorceress,
That many errant knights hath brought to wretchedness.

33.3 **Fradubio** *Fra[ter]* (L), "brother"; *dubio* (L), "doubt"
34.6 **As . . . suppress** as flames rage when one tries to suppress them

35]   In prime of youthly years, when courage hot
        The fire of love and joy of chivalry
        First kindled in my breast, it was my lot
        To love this gentle lady, whom ye see—
        Now not a lady, but a seeming tree;
        With whom as once I rode accompanied,
        Me chancéd of a knight encountered be,
        That had a like fair lady by his side,
        Like a fair lady, but did foul Duessa hide.

36]   Whose forgéd beauty he did take in hand
        All other dames to have exceeded far;
        I in defence of mine did likewise stand:
        Mine, that did then shine as the morning star;
        So both to battle fierce arrangéd are,
        In which his harder fortune was to fall
        Under my spear: such is the die of war;
        His lady, left as a prize martiál,
        Did yield her comely person, to be at my call.

37]   So doubly loved of ladies unlike fair—
        Th'one seeming such, the other such indeed—
        One day in doubt I cast for to compare,
        Whether in beauty's glory did exceed;
        A rosy garland was the victor's meed:
        Both seemed to win, and both seemed won to be,
        So hard the discord was to be agreed.
        Fraelissa was as fair as fair mote be,
        And ever false Duessa seemed as fair as she.

38]   The wicked witch, now seeing all this while
        The doubtful balance equally to sway,
        What not by right, she cast to win by guile,
        And by her hellish science raised straightway
        A foggy mist, that overcast the day,
        And a dull blast, that breathing on her face,
        Dimmed her former beauty's shining ray,

35.1 **courage** probably the older sense of heart, mind, spirit
37.4 **Whether** which   .6 **won** overcome   .8 **Fraelissa** prob-
ably "frailness"   38.6 **her** Fraelissa

And with foul ugly form did her disgrace:
Then was she fair alone, when none was fair in place.

39] Then cried she out: Fie, fie, deforméd wight,
Whose borrowed beauty now appeareth plain
To have before bewitchéd all men's sight;
O leave her soon, or let her soon be slain!
Her loathly visage viewing with disdain,
Eftsoons I thought her such, as she me told,
And would have killed her; but with feignéd pain,
The false witch did my wrathful hand withhold;
So left her, where she now is turned to treen mold.

40] Thenceforth I took Duessa for my dame,
And in the witch unweeting joyed long time,
Ne ever wist but that she was the same,
Till on a day (that day is every prime,
When witches wont do penance for their crime)
I chanced to see her in her proper hue,
Bathing herself in origan and thyme:
A filthy foul old woman I did view,
That ever to have touched her, I did deadly rue.

41] Her nether parts misshapen, monstruous,
Were hid in water, that I could not see;
But they did seem more foul and hideous
Than woman's shape man would believe to be.
Thenceforth from her most beastly company
I gan refrain, in mind to slip away,
Soon as appeared safe opportunity:
For danger great, if not assured decay,
I saw before mine eyes, if I were known to stray.

42] The devilish hag by changes of my cheer
Perceived my thought; and drowned in sleepy night,
With wicked herbs and ointments did besmear
My body all, through charms and magic might,
That all my senses were bereavéd quite:

.9 she Duessa   39.9 **treen mold** the shape of a tree   40.2 **un-
weeting** unwittingly   .4 **prime** usually morning or spring; here
possibly early in the month, at the time of the full moon

Then brought she me into this desert waste,
And by my wretched lover's side me pight,
Where now enclosed in wooden walls full fast,
Banished from living wights, our weary days we waste.

43]   But how long time, said then the Elfin knight,
Are you in this misforméd house to dwell?
We may not change (quoth he) this evil plight,
Till we be bathéd in a living well;
That is the term prescribéd by the spell.
O how, said he, mote I that well out find,
That may restore you to your wonted weal?
Time and sufficéd fates to former kind
Shall us restore: none else from hence may us unbind.

44]   The false Duessa, now Fidessa hight,
Heard how in vain Fradubio did lament,
And knew well all was true. But the good knight,
Full of sad fear and ghastly dreriment,
When all this speech the living tree had spent,
The bleeding bough did thrust into the ground,
That from the blood he might be innocent,
And with fresh clay did close the wooden wound:
Then turning to his lady, dead with fear her found.

45]   Her seeming dead he found with feignéd fear,
As all unweeting of that well she knew,
And pained himself with busy care to rear
Her out of careless swoon. Her eyelids blue
And dimméd sight with pale and deadly hue
At last she up gan lift: with trembling cheer
Her up he took, too simple and too true,
And oft her kissed. At length, all passéd fear,
He set her on her steed, and forward forth did bear.

42.7 **pight** put   43.1 **Elfin** i.e., of the court of the Faerie
Queene   .4 **living well** baptism or God's grace, cf. Song of
Solomon 4:15, John 4:10   .7 **wonted weal** customary well-being
44.1 **hight** called   45.1 **with feignèd fear** describes Duessa, not
the knight   .7 **too . . . true** describes the knight, not Duessa

# Book II

## Canto xii

*In Book II*, Sir Guyon, *the champion of Temperance, is guided by a* palmer (*pilgrim*) *to the* Bower of Bliss; *in this garden of sensual temptation dwells the sorceress* Acrasia (*incontinence*), *who has been the ruin of many knights. Guyon has overcome difficulties and resisted many temptations on the way. The last obstacle seems to be the pack of wild beasts outside the garden, which the palmer pacifies with his magic staff; but the most seductive temptations remain within the garden walls.* [Eds.]

42] Thence passing forth, they shortly do arrive
Whereas the Bower of Bliss was situate;
A place picked out by choice of best alive
That Nature's work by Art can imitate:
In which whatever in this worldly state
Is sweet and pleasing unto living sense,
Or that may daintiest fantasy aggrate,
Was pouréd forth with plentiful dispense,
And made there to abound with lavish affluence.

43] Goodly it was encloséd round about,
As well their entered guests to keep within
As those unruly beasts to hold without;
Yet was the fence thereof but weak and thin:
Naught feared their force, that fortalice to win,
But Wisdom's power, and Temperance's might,
By which the mightiest things enforcéd been;
And eke the gate was wrought of substance light,
Rather for pleasure than for battery or fight.

42.7 **aggrate** gratify   43.5 **Naught . . . win** to win that fortified outwork, the strength of none was feared, except the power of wisdom and temperance

36

44]  It framéd was of precious ivory,
     That seemed a work of admirable wit;
     And therein all the famous history
     Of Jason and Medea was ywrit:
     Her mighty charms, her furious loving fit,
     His goodly conquest of the golden fleece,
     His falséd faith, and love too lightly flit,
     The wondered Argo, which in venturous peace
     First through the Euxine seas bore all the flower of Greece.

45]  Ye might have seen the frothy billows fry
     Under the ship, as thorough them she went,
     That seemed the waves were into ivory,
     Or ivory into the waves were sent;
     And otherwhere the snowy substance sprent
     With vermeil, like the boy's blood therein shed,
     A piteous spectacle did represent;
     And otherwhiles with gold besprinkeléd,
     It seemed th'enchanted flame which did Creüsa wed.

46]  All this and more might in that goodly gate
     Be read, that ever open stood to all
     Which thither came: but in the porch there sate
     A comely personage of stature tall
     And semblance pleasing, more than natural,
     That travelers to him seemed to entice;
     His looser garment to the ground did fall,
     And flew about his heels in wanton wise,
     Not fit for speedy pace or manly exercise.

47]  They in that place him Geniús did call:
     Not that celestial power to whom the care
     Of life, and generatión of all
     That lives, pertains in charge particular
     (Who wondrous things concerning our welfare,
     And strange phantoms doth let us oft foresee,

45.1 **fry** foam  .2 **thorough** through  .5 **sprent** sprinkled  .6
**boy's** Medea scattered parts of her murdered brother to delay
her father's pursuit  .9 **Creüsa** jealous Medea gave Creüsa,
Jason's bride-to-be, a wedding garment which burned her to death;
thus Creüsa "wed" the flame

And oft of secret ills bids us beware:
That is our Self, whom, though we do not see,
Yet each doth in himself it well perceive to be;

48]   Therefore a god him sage antiquity
Did wisely make, and good Agdistes call):
But this same was to that quite contrary,
The foe of life, that good envies to all,
That secretly doth us procure to fall,
Through guileful semblance which he makes us see.
He of this garden had the governal,
And Pleasure's porter was devised to be,
Holding a staff in hand for more formality.

49]   With divers flowers he daintily was decked,
And strewéd round about, and by his side
A mighty mazer bowl of wine was set,
As if it had to him been sacrified;
Wherewith all new-come guests he gratified:
So did he eke Sir Guyon passing by,
But he his idle courtesy defied,
And overthrew his bowl disdainfully,
And broke his staff, with which he charméd semblants sly.

50]   Thus being entered, they behold around
A large and spacious plain, on every side
Strewéd with pleasance, whose fair grassy ground
Mantled with green, and goodly beautified
With all the ornaments of Flora's pride,
Wherewith her mother Art, as half in scorn
Of niggard Nature, like a pompous bride
Did deck her, and too lavishly adorn,
When forth from virgin bower she comes in th'early morn.

51]   Thereto the heavens, always jovial,
Looked on them lovely, still in steadfast state,
Ne suffered storm nor frost on them to fall—
Their tender buds or leaves to violate—
Nor scorching heat, nor cold intemperate

49.4 **sacrified** consecrated   .9 **charméd semblants sly** conjured
up evil spirits   51.3 **Ne** neither, nor

T'afflict the creatures which therein did dwell:
But the mild air with season moderate
Gently attempered, and disposed so well,
That still it breathéd forth sweet spirit and wholesome
    smell.

52]  More sweet and wholesome than the pleasant hill
Of Rhodope, on which the nymph that bore
A giant babe, herself for grief did kill;
Or the Thessalian Tempe, where of yore
Fair Daphne Phoebus' heart with love did gore;
Or Ida, where the gods loved to repair,
Whenever they their heavenly bowers forlore;
Or sweet Parnasse, the haunt of Muses fair;
Or Eden self, if ought with Eden mote compare.

53]  Much wondered Guyon at the fair aspect
Of that sweet place, yet suffered no delight
To sink into his sense, nor mind affect,
But passéd forth, and looked still forward right,
Bridling his will, and mastering his might,
Till that he came unto another gate:
No gate, but like one, being goodly dight
With boughs and branches, which did broad dilate
Their clasping arms, in wanton wreathings intricate:

54]  So fashionéd a porch with rare device,
Arched overhead with an embracing vine,
Whose bunches, hanging down, seemed to entice
All passers by to taste their luscious wine,
And did themselves into their hands incline,
As freely offering to be gatheréd:
Some deep empurpled as the hyacinth,
Some as the ruby, laughing sweetly red,
Some like fair emeralds, not yet well ripenéd.

55]  And them amongst, some were of burnished gold,
So made by art, to beautify the rest,

52.2 **nymph**  a nymph called Rhodope, who bore a giant son to
the god Neptune   .9 **mote**  might

Which did themselves amongst the leaves enfold,
As lurking from the view of covetous guest,
That the weak boughs, with so rich load oppressed,
Did bow adown, as overburdenéd.
Under that porch a comely dame did rest,
Clad in fair weeds, but foul disorderéd,
And garments loose, that seemed unmeet for womanhead.

56]  In her left hand a cup of gold she held,
And with her right the riper fruit did reach,
Whose sappy liquor, that with fullness swelled,
Into her cup she scruzed, with dainty breach
Of her fine fingers, without foul empeach,
That so fair wine-press made the wine more sweet;
Thereof she used to give to drink to each
Whom passing by she happenéd to meet:
It was her guise, all strangers goodly so to greet.

57]  So she to Guyon offered it to taste;
Who taking it out of her tender hand,
The cup to ground did violently cast,
That all in pieces it was broken found,
And with the liquor stainéd all the land:
Whereat Excess exceedingly was wroth,
Yet no'te the same amend, ne yet withstand,
But suffered him to pass, all were she loath;
Who, nought regarding her displeasure, forward goeth.

58]  There the most dainty paradise on ground
Itself doth offer to his sober eye,
In which all pleasures plenteously abound,
And none does other's happiness envy:
The painted flowers, the trees upshooting high,
The dales for shade, the hills for breathing space,
The trembling groves, the crystal running by;
And that which all fair works doth most agrace,
The art which all that wrought appearéd in no place.

55.9 **-head** -hood   56.4 **scruzed** squeezed   .5 **empeach** soiling
57.7 **no'te** could not   .8 **all were she** although she was   58.7
**crystal** i.e., water

59] One would have thought (so cunningly the rude
  And scornéd parts were mingled with the fine)
  That Nature had for wantonness ensued
  Art, and that Art at Nature did repine;
  So striving each th'other to undermine,
  Each did the other's work more beautify:
  So differing both in wills, agreed in fine;
  So all agreed, through sweet diversity,
  This garden to adorn with all variety.

60] And in the midst of all a fountain stood,
  Of richest substance that on earth might be:
  So pure and shiny that the silver flood
  Through every channel running one might see;
  Most goodly it with curious imagery
  Was over-wrought, and shapes of naked boys,
  Of which some seemed with lively jollity
  To fly about, playing their wanton toys,
  Whilst others did themselves embay in liquid joys.

61] And over all, of purest gold was spread
  A trail of ivy in his native hue:
  For the rich metal was so coloréd
  That wight who did not well advised it view
  Would surely deem it to be ivy true:
  Low his lascivious arms adown did creep,
  That themselves dipping in the silver dew,
  Their fleecy flowers they tenderly did steep,
  Which drops of crystal seemed for wantonness to weep.

62] Infinite streams continually did well
  Out of this fountain, sweet and fair to see,
  The which into an ample laver fell,
  And shortly grew to so great quantity
  That like a little lake it seemed to be,
  Whose depth exceeded not three cubits height,
  That through the waves one might the bottom see,
  All paved beneath with jasper shining bright,
  That seemed the fountain in that sea did sail upright.

59.7 **in fine** in the end 60.8 **toys** games .9 **embay** bathe

63]   And all the margin roundabout was set
      With shady laurel trees, thence to defend
      The sunny beams, which on the billows beat,
      And those which therein bathéd mote offend.
      As Guyon happened by the same to wend,
      Two naked damsels he therein espied,
      Which therein bathing, seeméd to contend,
      And wrestle wantonly; ne cared to hide
      Their dainty parts from view of any which them eyed.

64]   Sometimes the one would lift the other quite
      Above the waters, and then down again
      Her plunge, as overmasteréd by might,
      Where both awhile would coveréd remain,
      And each the other from to rise restrain;
      The whiles their snowy limbs, as through a veil,
      So through the chrystal waves appearéd plain:
      Then suddenly both would themselves unhele,
      And th'amorous sweet spoils to greedy eyes reveal.

65]   As that fair star, the messenger of morn,
      His dewy face out of the sea doth rear—
      Or as the Cyprian goddess, newly born
      Of th'Ocean's fruitful froth, did first appear—
      Such seeméd they, and so their yellow hair
      Crystalline humour droppéd down apace.
      Whom such when Guyon saw, he drew him near,
      And somewhat gan relent his earnest pace:
      His stubborn breast gan secret pleasance to embrace.

66]   The wanton maidens him espying, stood
      Gazing a while at his unwonted guise;
      Then th'one her self low duckéd in the flood,
      Abashed, that her a stranger did avise:
      But th'other rather higher did arise,
      And her two lily paps aloft displayed,
      And all that might his melting heart entice
      To her delights, she unto him bewrayed:
      The rest, hid underneath, him more desirous made.

63.2 **defend** ward off   64.8 **unhele** uncover   65.3 **goddess**
Venus   66.4 **avise** see

67] With that, the other likewise up arose,
   And her fair locks, which formerly were bound
   Up in one knot, she low adown did loose;
   Which flowing long and thick, her clothed around,
   And th'ivory in golden mantle gowned:
   So that fair spectacle from him was reft,
   Yet that which reft it no less fair was found;
   So hid in locks and waves from looker's theft,
   Naught but her lovely face she for his looking left.

68] Withal she laughéd, and she blushed withal,
   That blushing to her laughter gave more grace,
   And laughter to her blushing, as did fall;
   Now when they spied the knight to slack his pace
   Them to behold, and in his sparkling face
   The secret signs of kindled lust appear,
   Their wanton merriments they did increase,
   And to him beckoned to approach more near,
   And showed him many sights that courage cold could
      rear.

69] On which, when gazing him the palmer saw,
   He much rebuked those wandering eyes of his,
   And, counselled well, him forward thence did draw.
   Now are they come nigh to the Bower of Bliss—
   Of her fond favorites so named amiss—
   When thus the palmer: Now Sir, well avise;
   For here the end of all our travail is:
   Here wones Acrasia, whom we must surprise;
   Else she will slip away, and all our drift despise.

70] Eftsoons they heard a most melodious sound
   Of all that mote delight a dainty ear,
   Such as at once might not on living ground,
   Save in this paradise, be heard elsewhere;
   Right hard it was, for wight which did it hear,
   To read what manner music that mote be:
   For all that pleasing is to living ear

68.9 **courage cold** unaroused feelings  69.5 **her** Acrasia's  .8
**wones** dwells  70.3 **at once** at one time

Was there consorted in one harmony—
Birds, voices, instruments, winds, waters: all agree.

71]   The joyous birds, shrouded in cheerful shade,
Their notes unto the voice attempered sweet;
Th'angelical soft trembling voices made
To th'instruments divine respondence meet;
The silver-sounding instruments did meet
With the bass murmur of the water's fall:
The water's fall, with difference discrete—
Now soft, now loud—unto the wind did call;
The gentle warbling wind low answeréd to all.

72]   There, whence that music seeméd heard to be,
Was the fair witch, herself now solacing
With a new lover, whom through sorcery
And witchcraft, she from far did thither bring;
There she had him now laid a-slumbering,
In secret shade, after long wanton joys:
Whilst round about them pleasantly did sing
Many fair ladies, and lascivious boys,
That ever mixed their song with light licentious toys.

73]   And all that while, right over him she hung,
With her false eyes fast fixéd in his sight,
As seeking medicine whence she was stung,
Or greedily depasturing delight:
And oft inclining down with kisses light,
For fear of waking him, his lips bedewed,
And through his humid eyes did suck his spright,
Quite molten into lust and pleasure lewd;
Wherewith she sighéd soft, as if his case she rued.

74]   The whiles some one did chant this lovely lay:
Ah see, who so fair thing dost fain to see,
In springing flower the image of thy day;
Ah see the virgin rose, how sweetly she
Doth first peep forth with bashful modesty,

71.4 **meet** suitable  73.4 **depasturing** devouring, grazing  .7
**spright** spirit  74.2 **fain** desire

That fairer seems the less ye see her may;
Lo see soon after, how more bold and free
Her baréd bosom she doth broad display;
Lo see, soon after, how she fades and falls away.

75]　So passeth, in the passing of a day,
Of mortal life the leaf, the bud, the flower:
No more doth flourish, after first decay,
That erst was sought to deck both bed and bower
Of many a lady and many a paramour:
Gather therefore the rose, whilst yet is prime,
For soon comes age, that will her pride deflower:
Gather the rose of love, whilst yet is time,
Whilst loving thou mayest lovéd be with equal crime.

76]　He ceased, and then gan all the choir of birds
Their divers notes t'attune unto his lay,
As in approvance of his pleasing words.
The constant pair heard all that he did say,
Yet swervéd not, but kept their forward way
Through many covert groves and thickets close,
In which they creeping did at last display
That wanton lady, with her lover loose,
Whose sleepy head she in her lap did soft dispose.

77]　Upon a bed of roses she was laid,
As faint through heat, or dight to pleasant sin,
And was arrayed—or rather disarrayed—
All in a veil of silk and silver thin,
That hid no whit her alabaster skin,
But rather showed more white, if more might be:
More subtle web Arachne cannot spin,
Nor the fine nets, which oft we woven see
Of scorchéd dew, do not in th'air more lightly flee.

78]　Her snowy breast was bare to ready spoil
Of hungry eyes, which no'te therewith be filled,

75.6 **prime**　early in the day or year (morning or spring)　.9 **crime**
accountability　76.4 **pair** Guyon and the palmer　.6 **covert**
concealing　.7 **display** discover

And yet through languor of her late sweet toil,
Few drops, more clear than nectar, forth distilled,
That like pure orient pearls adown it trilled,
And her fair eyes sweet smiling in delight
Moistened their fiery beams, with which she thrilled
Frail hearts, yet quenchéd not; like starry light
Which sparkling on the silent waves does seem more
    bright.

79]  The young man sleeping by her seemed to be
Some goodly swain of honorable place,
That certes it great pity was to see
Him his nobility so foul deface;
A sweet regard, and amiable grace,
Mixéd with manly sternness, did appear
Yet sleeping in his well proportioned face,
And on his tender lips the downy hair
Did now but freshly spring, and silken blossoms bear.

80]  His warlike arms, the idle instruments
Of sleeping praise, were hung upon a tree,
And his brave shield, full of old monuments,
Was fouly razed, that none the signs might see;
Ne for them, ne for honor caréd he,
Ne aught that did to his advancement tend,
But in lewd loves, and wasteful luxury,
His days, his goods, his body he did spend:
O horrible enchantment, that him so did blend!

81]  The noble Elf and careful palmer drew
So nigh them (minding nought but lustful game)
That sudden forth they on them rushed, and threw
A subtle net, which only for the same
The skillful palmer formally did frame.
So held them under fast, the whiles the rest
Fled all away for fear of fouler shame.

80.3 **monuments** identifying marks, heraldic devices  .9 **blend**
may mean both blind and defile  81.1 **Elf** Guyon (a subject of
the Faerie Queene)  .2 **minding . . . game** Acrasia and her
lover thought only of lustful play  .5 **formally** appropriately

The fair enchantress, so unwares oppressed,
Tried all her arts, and all her sleights, thence out to wrest.

82]  And eke her lover strove: but all in vain;
For that same net so cunningly was wound,
That neither guile nor force might it distrain.
They took them both, and both them strongly bound
In captive bands, which there they ready found:
But her in chains of adamant he tied,
For nothing else might keep her safe and sound;
But Verdant (so he hight) he soon untied,
And counsel sage instead thereof to him applied.

83]  But all those pleasant bowers and palace brave
Guyon broke down, with rigor pitiless;
Nor aught their goodly workmanship might save
Them from the tempest of his wrathfulness,
But that their bliss he turned to balefulness;
Their groves he felled, their gardens did deface,
Their arbors spoil, their cabinets suppress,
Their banquet houses burn, their buildings raze:
And of the fairest late, now made the foulest place.

84]  Then led they her away; and eke that knight
They with them led, both sorrowful and sad:
The way they came, the same returned they right,
Till they arrivéd where they lately had
Charmed those wild beasts that raged with fury mad,
Which now awaking, fierce at them gan fly,
As in their mistress' rescue, whom they led;
But them the palmer soon did pacify.
Then Guyon asked what meant those beasts, which there
did lie.

85]  Said he: These seeming beasts are men indeed,
Whom this enchantress hath transformed thus:
Whilom her lovers, which her lusts did feed,
Now turnéd into figures hideous,
According to their minds like monstruous.

82.3 **distrain** tear off  .8 **hight** was called  83.7 **cabinets** summer houses  84.7 **they** Guyon and the palmer

—Sad end (quoth he) of life intemperate,
And mournful meed of joys deliciôus:
But, palmer, if it mote thee so aggrate,
Let them returnéd be unto their former state.

86]  Straightway he with his virtuous staff them struck,
And straight of beasts they comely men became;
Yet being men they did unmanly look,
And staréd ghastly, some for inward shame,
And some for wrath, to see their captive dame:
But one above the rest in speciál,
That had an hog been late, hight Grill by name,
Repinéd greatly, and did him miscall
That had from hoggish form him brought to natural.

87]  Said Guyon: See the mind of beastly man,
That hath so soon forgot the excellence
Of his creation when he life began,
That now he chooseth, with vile difference,
To be a beast, and lack intelligence.
To whom the palmer thus: The dunghill kind
Delights in filth and foul incontinence:
Let Grill be Grill, and have his hoggish mind,
But let us hence depart, whilst weather serves and wind.

85.8 **aggrate** gratify  86.8 **did him miscall** reviled him (the palmer)

# Book III

## Canto vi

*Book III, the book of chastity, contains many examples of this virtue, or of the lack of it. Two examples of chastity—the virgin and the chaste bride—are the twin sisters* Belphoebe *and* Amoret, *whose miraculous birth is recounted in Canto vi.* [Eds.]

4]   Her mother was the fair Chrysogonée
    (The daughter of Amphisa), who by race
    A Faery was, yborn of high degree.
    She bore Belphoebe; she bore in like case
    Fair Amoretta in the second place:
    These two were twins, and 'twixt them two did share
    The heritage of all celestial grace,
    That all the rest it seemed they robbéd bare
    Of bounty and of beauty, and all virtues rare.

5]   It were a goodly story to declare
    By what strange accident fair Chrysogone
    Conceived these infants, and how them she bare,
    In this wild forest wandering all alone,
    After she had nine months fulfilled and gone—
    For not as other women's common brood
    They were enwombéd in the sacred throne
    Of her chaste body, nor with common food,
    As other women's babes, they suckéd vital blood;

6]   But wondrously they were begot and bred
    Through influence of th'heavens fruitful ray,
    As it in antique books is mentionéd.
    It was upon a summer's shiny day,
    When Titan fair his beamés did display,
    In a fresh fountain, far from all men's view,
    She bathed her breast, the boiling heat t'allay;

6.5 **Titan** the sun

She bathed with roses red and violets blue,
And all the sweetest flowers that in the forest grew.

7]   Till faint through irksome weariness, adown
Upon the grassy ground herself she laid
To sleep, the whiles a gentle slumbering swoon
Upon her fell, all naked bare displayed;
The sunbeams bright upon her body played,
Being through former bathing mollified,
And pierced into her womb, where they embayed
With so sweet sense and secret power unspied,
That in her pregnant flesh they shortly fructified.

8]   Miraculous may seem to him that reads
So strange example of conceptión;
But reason teacheth that the fruitful seeds
Of all things living, through impressión
Of the sunbeams in moist complexión,
Do life conceive and quickened are by kind:
So after Nilus' inundatión,
Infinite shapes of creatures men do find
Enforméd in the mud on which the sun hath shined.

9]   Great father he of generatión
Is rightly called, th'author of life and light;
And his fair sister for creatión
Ministreth matter fit, which tempered right
With heat and humour, breeds the living wight.
So sprung these twins in womb of Chrysogone:
Yet wist she naught thereof, but sore affright,
Wondered to see her belly so upblown,
Which still increased till she her term had full outgone.

10]   Whereof conceiving shame and foul disgrace
(Albe her guiltless consciénce her cleared),
She fled into the wilderness a space,
Till that unwieldy burden she had reared,
And shunned dishonor, which as death she feared;
Where weary of long travel, down to rest

7.7 **embayed** bathed, suffused   8.7 **Nilus** the Nile   9.1 **he** the
sun   .3 **sister** the moon   10.2 **Albe** albeit, although   .6 **travel**
pun on *travail*

Herself she set, and comfortably cheered;
There a sad cloud of sleep her overcast,
And seizéd every sense with sorrow sore oppressed.

11]   It fortunéd, fair Venus having lost
Her little son, the winged god of love,
Who for some light displeasure which him crossed
Was from her fled, as flit as airy dove,
And left her blissful bower of joy above—
So from her often he had fled away,
When she for aught him sharply did reprove,
And wandered in the world in strange array,
Disguised in thousand shapes, that none might him
     bewray—

12]   Him for to seek, she left her heavenly house—
The house of goodly forms and fair aspects,
Whence all the world derives the glorious
Features of beauty, and all shapes select
With which high God his workmanship hath decked—
And searchéd every way, through which his wings
Had borne him, or his track she mote detect:
She promised kisses sweet, and sweeter things,
Unto the man that of him tidings to her brings.

13]   First she him sought in court, where most he used
Whilom to haunt, but there she found him not;
But many there she found which sore accused
His falsehood, and with foul infamous blot
His cruel deeds and wicked wiles did spot:
Ladies and lords she everywhere mote hear
Complaining how with his empoisoned shot
Their woeful hearts he wounded had whilere,
And so had left them languishing 'twixt hope and fear.

14]   She then the cities sought from gate to gate,
And everyone did ask, did he him see;
And everyone her answered, that too late
He had him seen, and felt the cruelty

11.3 **crossed** thwarted, made cross   .4 **flit** fleet, swift   13.8
**whilere** a while before

Of his sharp darts and hot artillery;
And everyone threw forth reproaches rife
Of his mischievous deeds, and said that he
Was the disturber of all civil life,
The enemy of peace, and author of all strife.

15]  Then in the country she abroad him sought,
And in the rural cottages inquired,
Where also many plaints to her were brought,
How he their heedless hearts with love had fired,
And his false venom through their veins inspired;
And eke the gentle shepherd swains, which sat
Keeping their fleecy flocks, as they were hired,
She sweetly heard complain, both how and what
Her son had to them done; yet she did smile thereat.

16]  But when in none of all these she him got,
She gan avise where else he mote him hide;
At last she her bethought that she had not
Yet sought the savage woods and forests wide,
In which full many lovely nymphs abide,
'Mongst whom might be that he did closely lie,
Or that the love of some of them him tied:
For-thy she thither cast her course t'apply,
To search the secret haunts of Diane's company.

17]  Shortly unto the wasteful woods she came,
Whereas she found the goddess with her crew,
After late chase of the embrewéd game,
Sitting beside a fountain in a rew,
Some of them washing with the liquid dew
From off their dainty limbs the dusty sweat
And soil which did deform their lively hue;
Others lay shaded from the scorching heat;
The rest upon her person gave attendance great.

18]  She, having hung upon a bough on high
Her bow and painted quiver, had unlaced

16.2 **avise** consider  .6 **closely** hidden, concealedly  .8 **for-thy**
therefore  17.1 **wasteful** desolate  .3 **embrewed** bloodstained
.4 **rew** row  .9 **her** Diana's

Her silver buskins from her nimble thigh,
And her lank loins ungirt, and breasts unbraced,
After her heat the breathing cold to taste;
Her golden locks, that late in tresses bright
Embraided were for hindering of her haste,
Now loose about her shoulders hung undight,
And were with sweet ambrosia all besprinkled light.

19] Soon as she Venus saw behind her back,
She was ashamed to be so loose surprised,
And wax half wroth against her damsels slack
That had not her thereof before advised,
But suffered her so carelessly disguised
Be overtaken. Soon her garments loose
Upgathering, in her bosom she comprised,
Well as she might, and to the goddess rose,
Whiles all her nymphs did like a garland her enclose.

20] Goodly she gan fair Cytherea greet,
And shortly askéd her what cause her brought
Into that wilderness, for her unmeet,
From her sweet bowers, and beds with pleasures fraught:
That sudden change she strange adventure thought.
To whom half weeping, she thus answeréd,
That she her dearest son Cupido sought,
Who in his frowardness from her was fled;
That she repented sore to have him angeréd.

21] Thereat Diana gan to smile, in scorn
Of her vain plaint, and to her, scoffing, said:
Great pity sure, that ye be so forlorn
Of your gay son, that gives ye so good aid
To your disports: ill mote ye been apaid.
But she was more engrievéd, and replied:
Fair sister, ill beseems it to upbraid
A doleful heart with so disdainful pride;
The like that mine, may be your pain another tide.

18.4 **lank** slender  .7 **for hindering of** so as not to hinder
21.5 **apaid** pleased

22]  As you in woods and wanton wilderness
Your glory set, to chase the savage beasts,
So my delight is all in joyfulness,
In beds, in bowers, in banquets, and in feasts;
And ill becomes you, with your lofty crests,
To scorn the joy that Jove is glad to seek;
We both are bound to follow heaven's behests,
And tend our charges with obeisance meek:
Spare, gentle sister, with reproach my pain to eke.

23]  And tell me, if that ye my son have heard
To lurk amongst your nymphs in secret wise,
Or keep their cabins: much I am afeared
Lest he like one of them himself disguise,
And turn his arrows to their exercise:
So may he long himself full easy hide:
For he is fair and fresh in face and guise,
As any nymph (let it not be envied).
So saying, every nymph full narrowly she eyed.

24]  But Phoebe therewith sore was angeréd,
And sharply said: Go dame, go seek your boy
Where you him lately left, in Mars his bed;
He comes not here; we scorn his foolish joy,
Ne lend we leisure to his idle toy:
But if I catch him in this company,
By Stygian lake I vow—whose sad annoy
The gods do dread—he dearly shall abye;
I'll clip his wanton wings, that he no more shall fly.

25]  Whom whenas Venus saw so sore displeased,
She inly sorry was, and gan relent
What she had said: so her she soon appeased
With sugared words and gentle blandishment,
Which as a fountain from her sweet lips went,
And welléd goodly forth; that in short space
She was well pleased, and forth her damsels sent

22.5 **crests** uplifted heads, pride  24.1 **Phoebe** Diana  .3 **Mars his bed** the bed of Mars  .5 **toy** game  .8 **abye** pay the penalty

Through all the woods, to search from place to place
If any track of him or tidings they mote trace.

26] To search the god of love, her nymphs she sent
Throughout the wandering forest everywhere:
And after them herself eke with her went
To seek the fugitive, both far and near;
So long they sought, till they arrivéd were
In that same shady covert whereas lay
Fair Chrysogone in slumbery trance whilere:
Who in her sleep (a wondrous thing to say)
Unwares had borne two babes, as fair as springing day.

27] Unwares she them conceived, unwares she bore;
She bore withouten pain that she conceived
Withouten pleasure, ne her need implore
Lucina's aid: which when they both perceived,
They were through wonder nigh of sense bereaved,
And gazing each on other, naught bespake;
At last they both agreed, her, seeming grieved,
Out of her heavy swoon not to awake,
But from her loving side the tender babes to take.

28] Up they them took—each one a babe uptook—
And with them carried, to be fosteréd.
Dame Phoebe to a nymph her babe betook,
To be upbrought in perfect maidenhead,
And of herself her name Belphoebe read.
But Venus hers thence far away conveyed,
To be upbrought in goodly womanhead,
And in her little love's stead, which was strayed,
Her Amoretta called, to comfort her, dismayed.

29] She brought her to her joyous paradise,
Where most she wones when she on earth does dwell.
So fair a place as Nature can devise:
Whether in Paphos, or Cytheron hill,

26.3 **her** Venus  .7 **whilere** a while before  27.3 **ne her need**
nor did she need to  28.4 **-head** -hood  .5 **of . . . read** called
her Belphoebe after herself  29.2 **wones** dwells

Or it in Cnidus be, I wote not well;
But well I wote by trial that this same
All other pleasant places doth excel,
And calléd is by her lost lover's name,
The Garden of Adonis, far renowned by fame.

30] In that same garden all the goodly flowers
Wherewith Dame Nature doth her beautify,
And decks the garlands of her paramours,
Are fetched: there is the first seminary
Of all things that are born to live and die,
According to their kinds. Long work it were
Here to account the endless progeny
Of all the weeds that bud and blossom there;
But so much as doth need, must needs be counted here.

31] It sited was in fruitful soil of old,
And girt in with two walls on either side:
The one of iron, the other of bright gold,
That none might thorough break, nor overstride;
And double gates it had, which opened wide,
By which both in and out men moten pass;
Th'one fair and fresh, the other old and dried;
Old Geniús the porter of them was,
Old Geniús, the which a double nature has.

32] He letteth in, he letteth out to wend
All that to come into the world desire;
A thousand thousand naked babes attend
About him day and night, which do require
That he with fleshly weeds would them attire:
Such as him list, such as eternal fate
Ordainéd hath, he clothes with sinful mire,
And sendeth forth to live in mortal state,
Till they again return back by the hinder gate.

.5 **Cnidus** like those mentioned in line above, a place associated
with Venus 30.4 **seminary** nursery .8 **weeds** plants .9
**counted** recounted 31.4 **thorough** through .8 **Geniús:** see
II, xii, 47–48 32.4 **require** request

33] After that they again returnéd been,
    They in that garden planted be again,
    And grow afresh, as they had never seen
    Fleshly corruptión, nor mortal pain.
    Some thousand years so do they there remain,
    And then of him are clad with other hue,
    Or sent into the changeful world again,
    Till thither they return, where first they grew:
    So like a wheel around they run from old to new.

34] Ne needs there gardener to set or sow,
    To plant or prune: for of their own accord
    All things as they created were do grow,
    And yet remember well the mighty word
    Which first was spoken by th'Almighty Lord,
    That bade them to increase and multiply:
    Ne do they need with water of the ford
    Or of the clouds to moisten their roots dry:
    For in themselves eternal moisture they imply.

35] Infinite shapes of creatures there are bred,
    And uncouth forms, which none yet ever knew,
    And every sort is in a sundry bed
    Set by itself, and ranked in comely rew:
    Some fit for reasonable souls t'endue,
    Some made for beasts, some made for birds to wear,
    And all the fruitful spawn of fishes' hue
    In endless ranks along enrangéd were,
    That seemed the oceán could not contain them there.

36] Daily they grow, and daily forth are sent
    Into the world, it to replenish more;
    Yet is the stock not lessenéd, nor spent,
    But still remains in everlasting store,
    As it at first created was of yore.
    For in the wide womb of the world there lies,
    In hateful darkness and in deep horror,
    An huge eternal Chaos, which supplies
    The substances of Nature's fruitful progenies.

34.9 **imply** contain    35.3 **sundry** separate

37]  All things from thence do their first being fetch,
     And borrow matter whereof they are made,
     Which whenas form and feature it does catch,
     Becomes a body, and doth then invade
     The state of life, out of the grisly shade.
     That substance is eterne, and bideth so—
     Ne when the life decays, and form does fade,
     Doth it consume, and into nothing go,
     But changéd is, and often altered to and fro.

38]  The substance is not changed, nor alteréd,
     But th'only form and outward fashión;
     For every substance is conditionéd
     To change her hue, and sundry forms to don,
     Meet for her temper and complexión:
     For forms are variable and decay,
     By course of kind, and by occasión;
     And that fair flower of beauty fades away,
     As doth the lily fresh before the sunny ray.

39]  Great enemy to it, and t' all the rest
     That in the Garden of Adonis springs,
     Is wicked Time, who with his scythe addressed,
     Does now the flowering herbs and goodly things,
     And all their glory to the ground down flings,
     Where they do wither, and are foully marred:
     He flies about, and with his flaggy wings
     Beats down both leaves and buds without regard,
     Ne ever pity may relent his malice hard.

40]  Yet pity often did the gods relent,
     To see so fair things marred and spoiléd quite:
     And their great mother Venus did lament
     The loss of her dear brood, her dear delight;
     Her heart was pierced with pity at the sight
     When, walking through the garden, them she saw,

37.8 **doth it consume** is it consumed   38.2 **th'only** only the
.3 **conditionéd** required   .7 **occasión** need   39.3 **addressed**
equipped, or ready   .7 **flaggy** drooping   .9 **may . . . malice**
may cause his malice to relent   40.1 **did** made

Yet no'te she find redress for such despite.
For all that lives, is subject to that law:
All things decay in time, and to their end do draw.

41] But were it not that Time their troubler is,
All that in this delightful garden grows
Should happy be, and have immortal bliss;
For here all plenty and all pleasure flows,
And sweet love gentle fits amongst them throws,
Without fell rancor, or fond jealousy;
Frankly each paramour his leman knows,
Each bird his mate, ne any does envy
Their goodly merriment and gay felicity.

42] There is continual spring, and harvest there
Continual, both meeting at one time:
For both the boughs do laughing blossoms bear
And with fresh colors deck the wanton prime,
And eke at once the heavy trees they climb,
Which seem to labor under their fruit's load;
The whiles the joyous birds make their pastime
Amongst the shady leaves, their sweet abode,
And their true loves without suspicion tell abroad.

43] Right in the middest of that paradise
There stood a stately mount, on whose round top
A gloomy grove of myrtle trees did rise,
Whose shady boughs sharp steel did never lop,
Nor wicked beasts their tender buds did crop;
But like a garland compasséd the height,
And from their fruitful sides sweet gum did drop,
That all the ground, with precious dew bedight,
Threw forth most dainty odors and most sweet delight.

44] And in the thickest covert of that shade
There was a pleasant arbor—not by art,
But of the trees' own inclination made—
Which knitting their rank branches part to part,
With wanton ivy twine entrailed athwart,
And eglantine and caprifole among,

42.4 **prime** spring .5 **they** the people of the garden 44.6
**caprifole** honeysuckle

Fashioned above within their inmost part,
That neither Phoebus' beams could through them throng,
Nor Aeolus' sharp blast could work them any wrong.

45] And all about grew every sort of flower
To which sad lovers were transformed of yore:
Fresh Hyacinthus, Phoebus' paramour,
And dearest love;
Foolish Narcisse, that likes the wat'ry shore;
Sad Amaranthus, made a flower but late—
Sad Amaranthus, in whose purple gore
Me seems I see Amintas' wretched fate,
To whom sweet poets' verse hath given endless date.

46] There wont fair Venus often to enjoy
Her dear Adonis' joyous company,
And reap sweet pleasure of the wanton boy;
There yet, some say, in secret he does lie,
Lappéd in flowers and precious spicery,
By her hid from the world, and from the skill
Of Stygian gods, which do her love envy;
But she herself, whenever that she will,
Possesseth him, and of his sweetness takes her fill.

47] And sooth it seems they say; for he may not
Forever die, and ever buried be
In baleful night, where all things are forgot:
Albe he subject to mortality,
Yet is eterne in mutability,
And by succession made perpetual,
Transforméd oft, and changéd diversly;
For him the father of all forms they call;
Therefore needs mote he live, that living gives to all.

48] There now he liveth in eternal bliss,
'Joying his goddess, and of her enjoyed:
Ne feareth he henceforth that foe of his,
Which with his cruel tusk him deadly cloyed:
For that wild boar, the which him once annoyed,

45.8 **Amintas** probably a reference to Sir Philip Sidney   48.4
**cloyed** gored

She firmly hath imprisonéd for aye,
That her sweet love his malice mote avoid,
In a strong rocky cave, which is, they say,
Hewn underneath that mount, that none him loosen may.

49] There now he lives in everlasting joy—
With many of the gods in company,
Which thither haunt—and with the winged boy
Sporting himself in safe felicity:
Who when he hath with spoils and cruelty
Ransacked the world, and in the woeful hearts
Of many wretches set his triumphs high,
Thither resorts, and laying his sad darts
Aside, with fair Adonis plays his wanton parts.

50] And his true love, fair Psyche, with him plays—
Fair Psyche, to him lately reconciled,
After long troubles and unmeet upbrays,
With which his mother Venus her reviled,
And eke himself her cruelly exiled:
But now in steadfast love and happy state
She with him lives, and hath him borne a child,
Pleasure, that doth both gods and men aggrate:
Pleasure, the daughter of Cupid and Psyche late.

51] Hither great Venus brought this infant fair,
The younger daughter of Chrysogonée,
And unto Psyche with great trust and care
Committed her, yfosteréd to be,
And trainéd up in true feminity;
Who no less carefully her tenderéd
Than her own daughter Pleasure, to whom she
Made her companion, and her lessonéd
In all the lore of love and goodly womanhead.

52] In which when she to perfect ripeness grew,
Of grace and beauty noble paragon,
She brought her forth into the worldés view,
To be th'example of true love alone,

49.5 **Who** Cupid   50.3 **upbrays** upbraidings, scoldings   .8 **aggrate** please   .9 **late** recent   51.6 **tenderéd** cared for

And lodestar of all chaste affectión
To all fair ladies that do live on ground.
To Faery court she came, where many one
Admired her goodly 'haviór, and found
His feeble heart wide launchéd with love's cruel wound.

53]   But she to none of them her love did cast—
Save to the noble knight Sir Scudamore,
To whom her loving heart she linkéd fast
In faithful love, t'abide for evermore,
And for his dearest sake enduréd sore,
Sore trouble of an heinous enemy,
Who her would forcéd have to have forlore
Her former love and steadfast loyalty—
As ye may elsewhere read that rueful history.

## Canto ix

*Two knights*, Sir Satyrane *and* Sir Paridell, *and a squire,
who are searching for shelter from a storm, find them-
selves at the gate of a castle. The squire tells the knights
that they will not be admitted to the castle because its old
master keeps all company away from his young wife.* [Eds.]

1]   Redoubted knights and honorable dames,
To whom I level all my labor's end,
Right sore I fear lest with unworthy blames
This odious argument my rhymes should shend
Or aught your goodly patiénce offend,
Whiles of a wanton lady I do write,
Which with her loose incontinence doth blend
The shining glory of your sovereign light,
And knighthood foul defacéd by a faithless knight.

2]   But never let th'example of the bad
Offend the good: for good by paragon
Of evil, may more notably be read,

**53.7 forlore** forsaken   **1.4 shend** put to shame   **.7 blend** defile
**2.2 paragon** comparison   **.3 read** perceived

As white seems fairer matched with black attone;
Ne all are shaméd by the fault of one:
For, lo, in heaven, whereas all goodness is,
Amongst the angels a whole legión
Of wicked sprights did fall from happy bliss;
What wonder then, if one, of women all, did mis?

3] Then listen, lordings, if ye list to weet
The cause why Satyrane and Paridell
Mote not be entertained, as seeméd meet,
Into that castle (as that squire does tell):
Therein a cankered crabbéd carl does dwell
That has no skill of court or courtesy,
Ne cares what men say of him, ill or well;
For all his days he drowns in privity—
Yet has full large to live and spend at liberty.

4] But all his mind is set on mucky pelf—
To hoard up heaps of evil gotten mass,
For which he others wrongs, and wrecks himself;
Yet is he linkéd to a lovely lass
Whose beauty doth her bounty far surpass,
The which to him both far unequal years
And also far unlike conditions has:
For she does joy to play amongst her peers,
And to be free from hard restraint and jealous fears.

5] But he is old, and witheréd like hay,
Unfit fair ladies' service to supply;
The privy guilt whereof makes him alway
Suspect her truth, and keep continual spy
Upon her with his other blinkéd eye;
Ne suffereth he resort of living wight
Approach to her, ne keep her company,
But in close bower her mews from all men's sight
Deprived of kindly joy and natural delight.

.4 **attone** at the same time  .8 **sprights** spirits  .9 **mis** amiss
3.1 **weet** know  .5 **carl** churl  .9 **full . . . live** ample means
4.5 **bounty** wealth, also virtue  5.5 **other** one is blind

6] Malbecco he, and Hellenore she hight,
   Unfitly yoked together in one team;
   That is the cause why never any knight
   Is suffered here to enter, but he seem
   Such as no doubt of him he need misdeem.
   Thereat Sir Satyrane gan smile, and say:
   Extremely mad the man I surely deem,
   That weens with watch and hard restraint to stay
   A woman's will which is disposed to go astray.

7] In vain he fears that which he cannot shun;
   For who wots not that woman's subtleties
   Can guilen Argus, when she list misdone?
   It is not iron bands, nor hundred eyes,
   Nor brazen walls, nor many wakeful spies
   That can withhold her wilful wandering feet;
   But fast good will, with gentle courtesies,
   And timely service to her pleasures meet,
   May her perhaps contain that else would algates fleet.

8] Then is he not more mad (said Paridell)
   That hath himself unto such service sold,
   In dolefull thralldom all his days to dwell?
   For sure a fool I do him firmly hold
   That loves his fetters, though they were of gold.
   But why do we devise of others ill,
   Whiles thus we suffer this same dotard old
   To keep us out, in scorn of his own will,
   And rather do not ransack all, and himself kill?

9] Nay; let us first (said Satyrane) entreat
   The man by gentle means to let us in;
   And afterwards affray with cruel threat,
   Ere that we to enforce it do begin:
   Then if all fail, we will by force it win,
   And eke reward the wretch for his misprize,
   As may be worthy of his heinous sin.

6.4 **but** unless   7.3 **guilen** beguile   .9 **algates** in any case
9.6 **misprize** scorn

That counsel pleased: then Paridell did rise,
And to the castle gate approached in quiet wise.

10] Whereat soft knocking, entrance he desired.
   The goodman self, which then the porter played,
   Him answeréd that all were now retired
   Unto their rest, and all the keys conveyed
   Unto their master, who in bed was laid,
   That none him durst awake out of his dream;
   And therefore them of patience gently prayed.
   Then Paridell began to change his theme,
   And threatened him with force and punishment extreme.

11] But all in vain, for naught mote him relent;
   And now so long before the wicket fast
   They waited, that the night was forward spent,
   And the fair welkin, foully overcast,
   Gan blowen up a bitter stormy blast,
   With shower and hail so horrible and dread
   That this fair meny were compelled at last
   To fly for succour to a little shed,
   The which beside the gate for swine was orderéd.

12] It fortunéd, soon after they were gone,
   Another knight, whom tempest thither brought,
   Came to that castle, and with earnest moan,
   Like as the rest, late entrance dear besought;
   But like so as the rest, he prayed for naught,
   For flatly he of entrance was refused;
   Sorely thereat he was displeased, and thought
   How to avenge himself so sore abused,
   And evermore the carl of courtesy accused.

13] But to avoid th'intolerable stour,
   He was compelled to seek some refuge near,
   And to that shed, to shroud him from the shower,
   He came, which full of guests he found whilere,

10.2 **goodman** master, Malbecco **played** pretended to be
11.2 **fast** fastened .7 **meny** group 12.4 **dear** earnestly .9
**carl** Malbecco **courtesy** i.e., lack of courtesy 13.1 **stour**
storm .4 **whilere** already

So as he was not let to enter there:
Whereat he gan to wax exceeding wroth,
And swore that he would lodge with them yfere,
Or them dislodge, all were they lief or loath;
And so defied them each, and so defied them both.

14]   Both were full loath to leave that needful tent,
And both full loath in darkness to debate;
Yet both full lief him lodging to have lent,
And both full lief his boasting to abate;
But chiefly Paridell his heart did grate
To hear him threaten so despitefully,
As if he did a dog in kennel rate
That durst not bark; and rather had he die,
Than, when he was defied, in coward corner lie.

15]   Tho hastily remounting to his steed,
He forth issued: like as a boisterous wind,
Which in th'earth's hollow caves hath long been hid,
And shut up fast within her prisons blind,
Makes the huge element against her kind
To move, and tremble as it were aghast,
Until that it an issue forth may find;
Then forth it breaks, and with his furious blast
Confounds both land and seas, and skies doth overcast.

16]   Their steel-head spears they strongly couched, and met
Together with impetuous rage and force:
That with the terror of their fierce affret,
They rudely drove to ground both man and horse,
That each awhile lay like a senseless corse.
But Paridell, sore bruiséd with the blow,
Could not arise, the counterchange to scorse,
Till that young squire him rearéd from below;
Then drew he his bright sword, and gan about him throw.

17]   But Satyrane forth stepping, did them stay
And with fair treaty pacified their ire;
Then when they were accorded from the fray,

.7 **yfere** together   14.5 **grate** fret   .7 **rate** berate   15.1 **tho**
then   16.3 **affret** encounter   .7 **scorse** exchange

Against that castle's lord they gan conspire,
To heap on him due vengeance for his hire.
They been agreed, and to the gates they go
To burn the same with unquenchable fire,
And that uncourteous carl, their common foe,
To do foul death to die, or wrap in grievous woe.

18] Malbecco, seeing them resolved indeed
To flame the gates, and hearing them to call
For fire in earnest, ran with fearful speed;
And to them calling from the castle wall,
Besought them humbly, him to bear withal,
As ignorant of servants' bad abuse
And slack attendance unto strangers' call.
The knights were willing all things to excuse
(Though naught believed), and entrance late did not
   refuse.

19] They been ybrought into a comely bower,
And served of all things that mote needful be;
Yet secretly their host did on them lower,
And welcomed more for fear, than charity;
But they dissembled what they did not see,
And welcoméd themselves. Each gan undight
Their garments wet, and weary armor free,
To dry themselves by Vulcan's flaming light,
And eke their lately bruiséd parts to bring in plight.

20] And eke that stranger knight, amongst the rest
Was for like need enforced to disarray:
Tho whenas veiléd was her loftly crest,
Her golden locks, that were in trammels gay
Upbounden, did themselves adown display,
And raught unto her heels; like sunny beams,
That in a cloud their light did long time stay,
Their vapor vaded, show their golden gleams,
And through the persant air shoot forth their azure
   streams.

19.5 **dissembled . . . see** pretended not to notice lack of
hospitality  .9 **plight** good condition  20.6 **raught** reached
.8 **vaded** gone  9 **persant** piercing  .9 **azure** like the sky

21]    She also doffed her heavy habergeon,
       Which the fair feature of her limbs did hide,
       And her well plighted frock, which she did wone
       To tuck about her short, when she did ride,
       So low let fall, that flowed from her lank side
       Down to her foot, with careless modesty.
       Then of them all she plainly was espied
       To be a woman wight, unwist to be:
       The fairest woman wight that ever eye did see.


22]    Like as Minerva, being late returned
       From slaughter of the Giants conqueréd—
       Where proud Encelade, whose wide nostrils burned
       With breathéd flames, like to a furnace red,
       Transfixéd with the spear, down tumbled dead
       From top of Hemus, by him heapéd high—
       Hath loosed her helmet from her lofty head,
       And her Gorgonian shield gins to untie
       From her left arm, to rest in glorious victory.


23]    Which, whenas they beheld, they smitten were
       With great amazement of so wondrous sight,
       And on each other, and they all on her
       Stood gazing, as if sudden great affright
       Had them surprised. At last, avising right
       Her goodly personage and glorious hue,
       Which they so much mistook, they took delight
       In their first error, and yet still anew
       With wonder of her beauty fed their hungry view.


24]    Yet no'te their hungry view be satisfied,
       But seeing, still the more desired to see,
       And ever firmly fixéd did abide
       In contemplation of divinity;
       But most they marveled at her chivalry,

---

21.3 **plighted** made   **did wone** was accustomed   .5 **lank** slen-
der   .6 **careless** carefree   .8 **unwist** unknown   22.3 **Encelade**
a giant   .6 **Hemus** Mt. Etna (?)   23.5 **avising** estimating
24.1 **no'te** could not

And noble prowess, which they had approved:
That much they fained to know who she mote be,
Yet none of all them here thereof amoved,
Yet every one her liked, and every one her loved.

25] And Paridell, though partly discontent
With his late fall and foul indignity,
Yet was soon won his malice to relent,
Through gracióus regard of her fair eye
And knightly worth, which he too late did try,
Yet triéd did adore. Supper was dight;
Then they Malbecco prayed, of courtesy,
That of his lady they might have the sight,
And company at meat, to do them more delight.

26] But he, to shift their curious request,
Gan causen, why she could not come in place:
Her craséd health, her late recourse to rest,
And humid evening, ill for sick folks' case:
But none of those excuses could take place,
Ne would they eat, till she in presence came.
She came in presence with right comely grace,
And fairly them saluted, as became,
And showed herself in all a gentle, courteous dame.

27] They sat to meat, and Satyrane his chance
Was her before, and Paridell beside;
But he himself sat looking still askance
Gainst Britomart, and ever closely eyed
Sir Satyrane, that glances might not glide:
But his blind eye, that sided Paridell,
All his demeanor from his sight did hide:
On her fair face so did he feed his fill,
And sent close messages of love to her at will.

.6 **approved** experienced  .8 **amoved** asked about  25.5 **late did try** recently tested  26.2 **causen** give excuses  .5 **take place** work  27.1–2 **his . . . before** happened to sit in front of her (Hellenore)  .3 **he** Malbecco  .4 **Britomart** the lady knight  .7 **his** Paridell's

28]   And ever and anon, when none was ware,
       With speaking looks, that close embassage bore,
       He roved at her, and told his secret care:
       For all that art he learnéd had of yore.
       Ne was she ignorant of that lewd lore,
       But in his eye his meaning wisely read,
       And with the like him answered evermore;
       She sent at him one fiery dart, whose head
       Empoisoned was with privy lust and jealous dread.

29]   He from that deadly throw made no defence,
       But to the wound his weak heart opened wide:
       The wicked engine, through false influence,
       Passed through his eyes, and secretly did glide
       Into his heart, which it did sorely gride.
       But nothing new to him was that same pain,
       Ne pain at all; for he so oft had tried
       The power thereof, and loved so oft in vain,
       That thing of course he counted, love to entertain.

30]   Thenceforth to her he sought to intimate
       His inward grief, by means to him well known:
       Now Bacchus' fruit out of the silver-plate
       He on the table dashed, as overthrown,
       Or of the fruitful liquor overflown,
       And by the dancing bubbles did divine,
       Or therein write to let his love be shown;
       Which well she read out of the learned line,
       A sacrament profane in mystery of wine.

31]   And when so of his hand the pledge she raught,
       The guilty cup she feignéd to mistake,
       And in her lap did shed her idle draught,
       Showing desire her inward flame to slake:
       By such close signs they secret way did make
       Unto their wills, and one eye's watch escape:

28.3 **roved** shot (glances)   29.5 **gride** pierce   .9 **of . . .
counted** he considered it a matter of course   30.3 **fruit** wine
31.1 **raught** took from him the offered (pledged) cup

Two eyes him needeth, for to watch and wake,
Who lovers will deceive. Thus was the ape,
By their fair handling, put into Malbecco's cape.

32] Now when of meats and drinks they had their fill,
Purpose was movéd by that gentle dame
Unto those knights adventurous, to tell
Of deeds of arms, which unto them became,
And every one his kindred and his name.
Then Paridell, in whom a kindly pride
Of gracious speech and skill his words to frame
Abounded, being glad of so fit tide
Him to commend to her, thus spake, of all well eyed:

33] Troy, that art now naught but an idle name,
And in thine ashes buried low dost lie,
Though whilom far much greater than thy fame,
Before that angry gods and cruel sky
Upon thee heaped a direful destiny,
What boots it boast thy glorious descent,
And fetch from heaven thy great genealogy—
Since all thy worthy praises being blent,
Their offspring hath embased, and later glory shent.

34] Most famous worthy of the world, by whom
That war was kindled, which did Troy inflame,
And stately towers of Ilion whilom
Brought into baleful ruin, was by name
Sir Paris, far renowned through noble fame:
Who through great prowess and bold hardiness,
From Lacedaemon fetched the fairest dame
That ever Greece did boast, or knight possess,
Whom Venus to him gave for meed of worthiness.

35] Fair Helen, flower of beauty excellent,
And garland of the mighty conquerors,
That madest many ladies dear lament
The heavy loss of their brave paramours,
Which they far off beheld from Trojan towers,

.8–9 **ape . . . cape** i.e., they made a monkey of him  32.6
**kindly** natural  33.8 **blent** stained  .9 **embased** made base
35.3 **dear** dearly

And saw the fields of fair Scamander strown
With carcasses of noble warriórs,
Whose fruitless lives were under furrow sown,
And Xanthus' sandy banks with blood all overflown.

36]   From him my lineage I derive aright,
Who long before the ten years' siege of Troy,
Whiles yet on Ida he a shepherd hight,
On fair Oenone got a lovely boy,
Whom for remembrance of her passéd joy,
She of his father *Parius* did name;
Who, after Greeks did Priam's realm destroy,
Gathered the Trojan relics saved from flame,
And with them sailing thence, to th'isle of Paros came.

\*     \*     \*

52]   But all the while that he these speeches spent,
Upon his lips hung fair dame Hellenore,
With vigilant regard, and due attent,
Fashioning worlds of fancies evermore
In her frail wit, that now her quite forlore:
The whiles unwares away her wondering eye
And greedy ears her weak heart from her bore;
Which he perceiving, ever privily
In speaking many false belgards at her let fly.

53]   So long these knights discourséd diversly
Of strange affairs and noble hardiment,
Which they had passed with mickle jeopardy,
That now the humid night was farforth spent,
And heavenly lamps were halfendale ybrent:
Which th'old man seeing well, who too long thought
Every discourse and every argument—
Which by the hours he measuréd—besought
Them go to rest. So all unto their bowers were brought.

6. **strown** strewn   36.3 **hight** was called   52.5 **forlore** deserted
(her)   .9 **belgards** sweet glances   53.5 **halfendale ybrent** half
burned down

## Canto x

1] The morrow next, so soon as Phoebus' lamp
   Bewrayéd had the world with early light,
   And fresh Aurora had the shady damp
   Out of the goodly heaven amoved quite,
   Fair Britomart and that same Faery knight
   Uprose, forth on their journey for to wend:
   But Paridell complained that his late fight
   With Britomart so sore did him offend,
   That ride he could not, till his hurts he did amend.

2] So forth they fared; but he behind them stayed,
   Maugre his host, who grudgéd grievously
   To house a guest that would be needs obeyed,
   And of his own him left not liberty:
   Might wanting measure moveth surquedry.
   Two things he fearéd (but the third was death):
   That fierce young man's unruly mastery;
   His money, which he loved as living breath;
   And his fair wife, whom honest long he kept unneth.

3] But patiénce perforce he must abye—
   What fortune and his fate on him will lay—
   Fond is the fear that finds no remedy;
   Yet warily he watcheth every way
   By which he feareth evil happen may:
   So th'evil thinks by watching to prevent;
   Ne doth he suffer her—nor night, nor day—
   Out of his sight herself once to absent.
   So doth he punish her, and eke himself torment.

4] But Paridell kept better watch than he,
   A fit occasion for his turn to find:
   False Love, why do men say thou canst not see,

---

1.5 **knight** Satyrane  2.5 **surquedry** presumption (Malbecco
feared Paridell might take advantage of his superior strength and
position)  .6 **fearéd** feared for  .9 **unneth** hardly  3.1 **abye**
endure

And in their foolish fancy feign thee blind,
That with thy charms the sharpest sight dost bind,
And to thy will abuse? Thou walkest free,
And seést every secret of the mind;
Thou seést all, yet none at all sees thee;
All that is by the working of thy deity.

5]   So perfect in that art was Paridell,
That he Malbecco's halven eye did wile,
His halven eye he wiléd wondrous well,
And Hellenore's both eyes did eke beguile:
Both eyes and heart at once, during the while
That he there sojournéd his wounds to heal;
That Cupid self it seeing, close did smile,
To weet how he her love away did steal,
And bade that none their joyous treason should reveal.

6]   The learnéd lover lost no time nor tide
That least advantage mote to him afford,
Yet bore so fair a sail that none espied
His secret drift, till he her laid aboard.
When so in open place, and common board,
He fortuned her to meet, with common speech
He courted her, yet baited every word,
That his ungentle host no'te him appeach
Of vile ungentleness, or hospitage's breach.

7]   But when apart (if ever her apart)
He found, then his false engines fast he plied,
And all the sleights unbosomed in his heart;
He sighed, he sobbed, he swooned, he perdie died,
And cast himself on ground her fast beside:
Tho when again he him bethought to live,
He wept, and wailed, and false laments belied,
Saying but if she mercy would him give
That he mote algates die, yet did his death forgive.

5.2 **halven eye** half sight (he has only half his eyesight   .8
**weet** know   6.5 **when so** whenever      **board** dining table
7.8 **but if** unless   .9 **algates** altogether

8] And otherwhiles, with amorous delights
   And pleasing toys he would her entertain;
   Now singing sweetly, to surprise her sprights,
   Now making lays of love and lovers' pain—
   Bransles, ballades, virelays, and verses vain;
   Oft purposes, oft riddles he devised,
   And thousands like, which flowéd in his brain,
   With which he fed her fancy, and enticed
   To take to his new love, and leave her old despised.

9] And everywhere he might, and every while,
   He did her service dutiful, and sued
   At hand with humble pride and pleasing guile,
   So closely yet that none but she it viewed,
   Who well perceivéd all, and all endued.
   Thus finely did he his false net dispread,
   With which he many weak hearts had subdued
   Of yore, and many had alike misled:
   What wonder then, if she were likewise carriéd?

10] No fort so 'fensible, no walls so strong,
    But that continual battery will rive,
    Or daily siege, through dispurveyance long
    And lack of rescues, will to parley drive;
    And peace, that unto parley ear will give,
    Will shortly yield itself, and will be made
    The vassal of the victor's will belive.
    That stratagem had oftentimes assayed
    This crafty paramour, and now it plain displayed.

11] For through his trains he her entrappéd hath,
    That she her love and heart hath wholly sold
    To him, without regard of gain, or scathe,
    Or care of credit, or of husband old,
    Whom she hath vowed to dub a fair cuckold.
    Naught wants but time and place, which shortly she
    Deviséd hath, and to her lover told.

8.5 **Bransles** songs for dancing  .6 **purposes** question games
9.5 **endued** took (it) in  10.3 **dispurveyance** lack of provi-
sions  .7 **belive** quickly  11.1 **trains** tricks

It pleaséd well. So well they both agree;
So ready ripe to ill, ill women's counsels be.

12] Dark was the evening, fit for lovers' stealth,
When chanced Malbecco busy be elsewhere;
She to his closet went, where all his wealth
Lay hid: thereof she countless sums did rear,
The which she meant away with her to bear;
The rest she fired for sport, or for despite,
As Helen, when she saw aloft appear
The Trojan flames, and reach to heaven's height,
Did clap her hands, and joyéd at that doleful sight.

13] This second Helen, fair dame Hellenore,
The whiles her husband ran with sorry haste
To quench the flames, which she had tined before,
Laughed at his foolish labor spent in waste,
And ran into her lover's arms right fast;
Where, straight embracéd, she to him did cry
And call aloud for help, ere help were past;
For lo that guest would bear her forcibly,
And meant to ravish her, that rather had to die.

14] The wretched man hearing her call for aid,
And ready seeing him with her to fly,
In his disquiet mind was much dismayed;
But when again he backward cast his eye,
And saw the wicked fire so furiously
Consume his heart, and scorch his idol's face,
He was therewith distresséd diversly,
Ne wist he how to turn, nor to what place:
Was never wretched man in such a woeful case.

15] Aye when to him she cried, to her he turned,
And left the fire; love money overcame:
But when he markéd, how his money burned,
He left his wife; money did love disclaim:
Both was he loath to lose his lovéd dame

12.4 **rear** take  13.3 **tined** kindled  .6 **him** Malbecco  .9
**rather had** would rather  14.2 **him** Paridell

And loath to leave his liefest pelf behind,
Yet sith he no'te save both, he saved that same
Which was the dearest to his dunghill mind,
The god of his desire, the joy of misers blind.

16] Thus whilst all things in troublous uproar were,
And all men busy to suppress the flame,
The loving couple need no rescue fear,
But leisure had, and liberty to frame
Their purposed flight, free from all men's reclaim;
And night, the patroness of love-stealth fair,
Gave them safe conduct, till to end they came:
So been they gone yfere, a wanton pair
Of lovers loosely knit, where list them to repair.

17] Soon as the cruel flames yslakéd were,
Malbecco, seeing how his loss did lie,
Out of the flames which he had quenched whilere
Into huge waves of grief and jealousy
Full deep emplungéd was, and drownéd nigh,
'Twixt inward dole and felonous despite;
He raved, he wept, he stamped, he loud did cry,
And all the passions that in man may light
Did him at once oppress, and vex his caitive spright.

18] Long thus he chewed the cud of inward grief,
And did consume his gall with anguish sore;
Still when he muséd on his late mischief,
Then still the smart thereof increaséd more,
And seemed more grievous than it was before:
At last when sorrow he saw booted naught,
Ne grief might not his love to him restore,
He gan devise how her he rescue mought;
Ten thousand ways he cast in his confuséd thought.

19] At last resolving like a pilgrim poor
To search her forth, where so she might be found,
And bearing with him treasure in close store,
The rest he leaves in ground; so takes in hand

16.9 **where . . . repair** wherever they wanted to go 17.6
**felonous** fierce .9 **spright** spirit

To seek her endlong, both by sea and land.
Long he her sought, he sought her far and near,
And everywhere that he might understand
Of knights and ladies any meetings were,
And of each one he met, he tidings did inquire.

20]  But all in vain; his woman was too wise
Ever to come into his couch again,
And he too simple ever to surprise
The jolly Paridell, for all his pain.
One day, as he forpasséd by the plain
With weary pace, he far away espied
A couple, seeming well to be his twain,
Which hovéd close under a forest side,
As if they lay in wait, or else themselves did hide.

21]  Well weenéd he that those the same mote be,
And as he better did their shape avise,
Him seeméd more their manner did agree:
For th'one was arméd all in warlike wise,
Whom to be Paridell he did devise;
And th'other all yclad in garments light,
Discolored like to womanish disguise,
He did resemble to his lady bright;
And ever his faint heart much yearnéd at the sight.

22]  And ever fain he towards them would go,
But yet durst not for dread approachen nigh,
But stood aloof, unweeting what to do;
Till that, pricked forth with love's extremity,
That is the father of foul jealousy,
He closely nearer crept, the truth to weet:
But, as he nigher drew, he easily
Might 'scern that it was not his sweetest sweet,
Nor yet her *bel amour*, the partner of his sheet.

23]  But it was scornful Braggadocchio,
That with his servant Trompart hovered there,
Since late he fled from his too earnest foe:

21.7  **discolored** multicolored   23.2  **Trompart** "deceiver"   .3
**foe** in an earlier canto, Braggadocchio has been put to flight by
a stranger knight

Whom such whenas Malbecco spiéd clear,
He turnéd back, and would have fled arear;
Till Trompart, running hastily, him did stay,
And bade before his sovereign lord appear:
That was him loath, yet durst he not gainsay,
And coming him before, low louted on the ley.

24] The boaster at him sternly bent his brow,
As if he could have killed him with his look,
That to the ground him meekly made to bow,
And awful terror deep into him struck,
That every member of his body quoke.
Said he: Thou man of naught, what dost thou here,
Unfitly furnished with thy bag and book,
Where I expected one with shield and spear,
To prove some deeds of arms upon an equal peer?

25] The wretched man at his imperious speech
Was all abashed, and low prostrating, said:
Good Sir, let not my rudeness be no breach
Unto your patience, ne be ill apaid;
For I unwares this way by fortune strayed,
A silly pilgrim driven to distress,
That seek a lady—There he sudden stayed,
And did the rest with grievous sighs suppress,
While tears stood in his eyes, few drops of bitterness.

26] What lady, man? (said Trompart) Take good heart,
And tell thy grief, if any hidden lie;
Was never better time to show thy smart
Than now, that noble succour is thee by,
That is the whole world's common remedy.—
That cheerful word his weak heart much did cheer,
And with vain hope his spirits faint supply,
That bold he said: O most redoubted peer,
Vouchsafe with mild regard a wretch's case to hear.

27] Then, sighing sore: It is not long (said he)
Since I enjoyed the gentlest dame alive;

.9 **louted** bowed **ley** lea, meadow  25.4 **apaid** pleased  .6
**silly** harmless

Of whom a knight—no knight at all perdie,
But shame of all, that do for honor strive—
By treacherous deceit did me deprive;
Through open outrage he her bore away,
And with foul force unto his will did drive,
Which all good knights that arms do bear this day
Are bound for to revenge, and punish if they may.

28]  And you, most noble lord, that can and dare
Redress the wrong of miserable wight,
Cannot employ your most victorious spear
In better quarrel than defence of right,
And for a lady 'gainst a faithless knight;
So shall your glory be advancéd much,
And all fair ladies magnify your might,
And eke myself, albe I simple such,
Your worthy pain shall well reward with guerdon rich.

29]  With that, out of his budget forth he drew
Great store of treasure, therewith him to tempt;
But he on it looked scornfully askew,
As much disdaining to be so misdempt,
Or a warmonger to be basely nempt;
And said, Thy offers base I greatly loathe,
And eke thy words uncourteous and unkempt;
I tread in dust thee and thy money both,
That, were it not for shame—so turned from him, wroth.

30]  But Trompart, that his master's humor knew
In lofty looks to hide a humble mind,
Was inly tickled with that golden view,
And in his ear him rownded close behind;
Yet stooped he not, but lay still in the wind,
Waiting advantage on the prey to seize;
Till Trompart, lowly to the ground inclined,
Besought him his great courage to appease,
And pardon simple man, that rash did him displease.

---

28.8 **simple such** (am) so simple   29.1 **budget** pouch   .4
**misdempt** misdeemed, misjudged   .5 **warmonger** mercenary
**nempt** called   30.4 **rownded** whispered   .5 **stooped . . . wind**
hovered over his intended victim

31] Big looking like a doughty doucepeer,
At last he thus: Thou clod of vilest clay,
I pardon yield, and with thy rudeness bear;
But weet henceforth, that all that golden prey,
And all else that the vain world vaunten may,
I loath as dung, nor deem my due reward:
Fame is my meed, and glory virtue's prey.
But minds of mortal men are muchel marred,
And moved amiss with massy muck's unmeet regard.

32] And more, I grant to thy great misery
Gracious respect; thy wife shall back be sent,
And that vile knight, whoever that he be,
Which hath thy lady reft, and knighthood shent
(By Sanglamort my sword, whose deadly dent
The blood hath of so many thousands shed,
I swear) ere long shall dearly it repent;
Ne he 'twixt heaven and earth shall hide his head,
But soon he shall be found, and shortly done be dead.

33] The foolish man thereat wax wondrous blithe,
As if the words so spoken were half done,
And humbly thankéd him a thousand sith,
That had from death to life him newly won.
Tho forth the boaster marching, brave begun
His stolen steed to thunder furiously,
As if he heaven and hell would overrun
And all the world confound with cruelty,
That much Malbecco joyéd in his company.

34] Thus long they three together traveléd,
Through many a wood and many an uncouth way,
To seek his wife, that was far wanderéd:
But those two sought naught but the present prey—
To wit the treasure, which he did bewray,
On which their eyes and hearts were wholly set,

31.1 **doucepeer** champion. .4 **prey** booty .9 **massy . . . regard** unfit regard for filthy lucre 32.4 **shent** shamed .5 **Sanglamort** "bloody death" 33.3 **sith** times .6 **stolen** from Sir Guyon 34.2 **uncouth** unknown .4 **two** Braggadocchio and Trompart

With purpose how they might it best betray;
For since the hour that first he did them let
The same behold, therewith their keen desires were whet.

35]  It fortunéd as they together fared,
They spied where Paridell came pricking fast
Upon the plain, the which himself prepared
To joust with that brave stranger knight a cast,
As on adventure by the way he passed:
Alone he rode without his paragon;
For having filched her bells, her up he cast
To the wide world, and let her fly alone:
He nould be clogged. So had he servéd many one.

36]  The gentle lady, loose at random left,
The greenwood long did walk, and wander wide
At wild adventure, like a forlorn weft,
Till on a day the satyrs her espied,
Straying alone withouten groom or guide;
Her up they took, and with them home her led,
With them as housewife ever to abide,
To milk their goats, and make them cheese and bread,
And every one as common good her handeléd.

37]  That shortly she Malbecco has forgot,
And eke Sir Paridell, all were he dear—
Who from her went to seek another lot,
And now by fortune was arrivéd here
Where those two guilers with Malbecco were;
Soon as the old man saw Sir Paridell,
He fainted, and was almost dead with fear,
Ne word he had to speak, his grief to tell,
But to him louted low, and greeted goodly well.

38]  And after askéd him for Hellenore.
I take no keep of her (said Paridell),

35.6 **paragon** mate  .7 **filched her bells** taken from her what
he wanted (like the bells from a trained hawk)  .9 **nould** would
not  36.3 **weft** waif  .9 **good** goods, possession  37.7 **fainted**
became faint

She woneth in the forest there before.
—So forth he rode, as his adventure fell;
The whiles the boaster from his lofty sell
Feigned to alight, something amiss to mend;
But the fresh swain would not his leisure dwell,
But went his way; whom when he passéd kenned,
He up remounted light, and after feigned to wend.

39]    Perdie nay (said Malbecco), shall ye not:
But let him pass as lightly as he came:
For little good of him is to be got,
And mickle peril to be put to shame.
But let us go to seek my dearest dame,
Whom he hath left in yonder forest wild;
For of her safety in great doubt I am,
Lest savage beasts her person have despoiled:
Then all the world is lost, and we in vain have toiled.

40]    They all agree, and forward them addressed.
Ah, but (said crafty Trompart) wit ye well
That yonder in that wasteful wilderness
Huge monsters haunt, and many dangers dwell;
Dragons, and minotaurs, and fiends of hell,
And many wild woodmen, which rob and rend
All travelers; therefore advise ye well,
Before ye enterprise that way to wend:
One may his journey bring too soon to evil end.

41]    Malbecco stopped in great astonishment,
And with pale eyes fast fixéd on the rest,
Their counsel craved in danger imminent.
Said Trompart: You that are the most oppressed
With burden of great treasure, I think best
Here for to stay in saféty behind;
My lord and I will search the wide forest.
That counsel pleaséd not Malbecco's mind,
For he was much afraid himself alone to find.

38.5 **sell** saddle  .7 **his leisure dwell** wait for him  .8 **he passéd kenned:** when Braggadocchio knew Paridell had passed by  40.3 **wasteful** desolate

42] Then is it best (said he) that ye do leave
    Your treasure here in some security,
    Either fast closéd in some hollow grave,
    Or buried in the ground from jeopardy,
    Till we return again in saféty:
    As for us two, lest doubt of us ye have,
    Hence far away we will blindfolded lie,
    Ne privy be unto your treasure's grave.
    It pleaséd: so he did. Then they march forward brave.

43] Now when amid the thickest woods they were,
    They heard a noise of many bagpipes shrill,
    And shrieking hubbubs them approaching near,
    Which all the forest did with horror fill:
    That dreadful sound the boaster's heart did thrill
    With such amazement that in haste he fled,
    Ne ever lookéd back for good or ill,
    And after him eke fearful Trompart sped;
    The old man could not fly, but fell to ground half dead.

44] Yet afterwards, close creeping as he might,
    He in a bush did hide his fearful head;
    The jolly satyrs, full of fresh delight,
    Came dancing forth, and with them nimbly led
    Fair Hellenore, with garlands all bespread,
    Whom their May-Lady they had newly made:
    She, proud of that new honor which they read,
    And of their lovely fellowship full glad,
    Danced lively, and her face did with a laurel shade.

45] The silly man that in the thicket lay
    Saw all this goodly sport, and grievéd sore,
    Yet durst he not against it do or say,
    But did his heart with bitter thoughts engore,
    To see th'unkindness of his Hellenore.
    All day they dancéd with great lustihead,
    And with their hornéd feet the green grass wore,
    The whiles their goats upon the browzes fed,
    Till drooping Phoebus gan to hide his golden head.

42.1 **he** Trompart   44.7 **read** decreed   45.4 **engore** wound
.6 **-head** -hood   .8 **browzes** shoots

46]  Tho up they gan their merry pipes to truss,
And all their goodly herds did gather round,
But every satyr first did give a buss
To Hellenore: so busses did abound.
Now gan the humid vapor shed the ground
With pearly dew, and th'earthés gloomy shade
Did dim the brightness of the welkin round,
That every bird and beast awarnéd made
To shroud themselves, whiles sleep their senses did invade.

47]  Which when Malbecco saw, out of his bush
Upon his hands and feet he crept full light,
And like a goat amongst the goats did rush,
That through the help of his fair horns on height,
And misty damp of misconceiving night,
And eke through likeness of his goatish beard,
He did the better counterfeit aright:
So home he marched amongst the hornéd herd,
That none of all the satyrs him espied or heard.

48]  At night, when all they went to sleep, he viewed
Whereas his lovely wife amongst them lay,
Embracéd of a satyr rough and rude,
Who all the night did mind his joyous play:
Nine times he heard him come aloft ere day,
That all his heart with jealousy did swell;
But yet that night's example did bewray
That not for naught his wife them loved so well,
When one so oft a night did ring his matins bell.

49]  So closely as he could, he to them crept,
When weary of their sport to sleep they fell,
And to his wife, that now full soundly slept,
He whispered in her ear, and did her tell
That it was he, which by her side did dwell,
And therefore prayed her wake, to hear him plain.
As one out of a dream not wakéd well,
She turned her, and returnéd back again;
Yet her for to awake he did the more constrain.

47.4 **horns** the traditional headgear of a cuckold   .5 **misconceiving** misleading   49.6 **plain** complain

50] At last, with irksome trouble she abrade,
And then perceiving that it was indeed
Her old Malbecco which did her upbraid
With looseness of her love and loathly deed,
She was astonished with exceeding dread,
And would have waked the satyr by her side;
But he her prayed, for mercy or for meed,
To save his life, nor let him be descried,
But harken to his lore, and all his counsel hide.

51] Tho gan he her persuade to leave that lewd
And loathsome life, of God and man abhorred,
And home return, where all should be renewed
With perfect peace and bands of fresh accord,
And she received again to bed and board
As if no trespass ever had been done:
But she it all refuséd at one word,
And by no means would to his will be won,
But chose among the jolly satyrs still to wone.

52] He wooéd her till day-spring he espied;
But all in vain: and then turned to the herd,
Who butted him with horns on every side,
And trod down in the dirt, where his hoar beard
Was foully dight, and he of death afeared.
Early before the heavens' fairest light
Out of the ruddy East was fully reared,
The herds out of their folds were looséd quite,
And he amongst the rest crept forth, in sorry plight.

53] So soon as he the prison door did pass,
He ran as fast as both his feet could bear,
And never lookéd, who behind him was,
Ne scarcely who before: like as a bear,
That creeping close amongst the hives to rear
A honeycomb, the wakeful dogs espy,
And him assailing, sore his carcass tear,

50.1 **abrade** awoke   51.9 **still** always   **wone** dwell

That hardly he with life away does fly,
Ne stays, till safe himself he see from jeopardy.

54] Ne stayed he, till he came unto the place
Where late his treasure he entombéd had,
Where when he found it not (for Trompart base
Had it purloinéd for his master bad)
With extreme fury he became quite mad,
And ran away, ran with himself away:
That who so strangely had him seen bestad,
With upstart hair and staring eyes' dismay,
From Limbo lake him late escapéd sure would say.

55] High over hills and over dales he fled,
As if the wind him on his wings had born,
Ne bank nor bush could stay him, when he sped
His nimble feet, as treading still on thorn:
Grief, and despite, and jealousy, and scorn
Did all the way him follow hard behind,
And he himself himself loathed so forlorn,
So shamefully forlorn of womankind:
That, as a snake, still lurkéd in his wounded mind.

56] Still fled he forward, looking backward still,
Ne stayed his flight nor fearful agony,
Till that he came unto a rocky hill,
Over the sea suspended dreadfully,
That living creature it would terrify
To look adown, or upward to the height:
From thence he threw himself dispiteously,
All desperate of his fore-damnéd spright,
That seemed no help for him was left in living sight.

57] But through long anguish and self-murdering thought
He was so wasted and forpinéd quite,
That all his substance was consumed to naught,
And nothing left, but like an airy spright
That on the rocks he fell so flit and light

54.7 **bestad**  situated   56.8 **fore-damnéd**  doomed to damnation
57.5 **flit**  insubstantial

That he thereby received no hurt at all,
But chancéd on a craggy cliff to light;
Whence he with crooked claws so long did crawl,
That at the last he found a cave with entrance small.

58]   Into the same he creeps, and thenceforth there
Resolved to build his baleful mansión,
In dreary darkness, and continual fear
Of that rock's fall, which ever and anon
Threats with huge ruin him to fall upon,
That he dare never sleep, but that one eye
Still ope he keeps for that occasión;
Ne ever rests he in tranquillity,
The roaring billows beat his bower so boistrously.

59]   Ne ever is he wont on aught to feed,
But toads and frogs, his pasture poisonous,
Which in his cold complexión do breed
A filthy blood, or humor rancorous,
Matter of doubt and dread suspicious,
That doth with cureless care consume the heart,
Corrupts the stomach with gall viciós,
Cross cuts the liver with internal smart,
And doth transfix the soul with death's eternal dart.

60]   Yet he can never die, but dying lives,
And doth himself with sorrow new sustain,
That death and pleasure turns to pleasing pain.
There dwells he ever, miserable swain,
Hateful, both to himself and every wight;
Where he through privy grief, and horror vain,
Is waxen so deformed that he has quite
Forgot he was a man, and Jealousy is hight.

59.2 **pasture** food   60.9 **hight** called

## Canto xi

1]  O hateful hellish snake, what fury first
    Brought thee from baleful house of Proserpine,
    Where in her bosom she thee long had nursed,
    And fostered up with bitter milk of tine,
    Foul Jealousy, that turnest love divine
    To joyless dread, and makest the loving heart
    With hateful thoughts to languish and to pine,
    And feed itself with self-consuming smart?
    Of all the passions in the mind thou vilest art.

2]  O let him far be banishéd away,
    And in his stead let Love forever dwell,
    Sweet Love, that doth his golden wings embay
    In blesséd nectar, and pure pleasure's well,
    Untroubled of vile fear, or bitter fell.
    And ye fair ladies, that your kingdoms make
    In th'hearts of men, them govern wisely well,
    And of fair Britomart example take,
    That was as true in love as turtle to her make.

> Britomart, *the champion of chastity, and true love, finds*
> Scudamore. *He tells her of* Amoret's *abduction by the*
> *enchanter* Busirane. *Scudamore cannot free Amoret, but*
> *Britomart can, and does so.* [Eds.]

7]  Fair Britomart so long him followéd
    That she at last came to a fountain sheer,
    By which there lay a knight all wallowéd
    Upon the grassy ground, and by him near
    His habergeon, his helmet, and his spear;
    A little off, his shield was rudely thrown,
    On which the wingéd boy in colors clear

1.4 **tine** anger  2.3 **embay** bathe  .5 **fell** rancor  .9 **turtle**
turtledove  **make** mate

Depicted was, full easy to be known,
And he thereby, wherever it in field was shown.

8] His face upon the ground did groveling lie,
As if he had been slumbering in the shade,
That the brave maid would not, for courtesy,
Out of his quiet slumber him abrade,
Nor seem too suddenly him to invade:
Still as she stood, she heard with grievous throb
Him groan, as if his heart were pieces made,
And with most painful pangs to sigh and sob,
That pity did the virgin's heart of patience rob.

9] At last forth breaking into bitter plaints
He said: O sovereign Lord that sitt'st on high,
And reignst in bliss amongst thy blessed saints,
How suffrest thou such shameful cruelty,
So long unwreakéd of thine enemy?
Or hast thou, Lord, of good men's cause no heed?
Or doth thy justice sleep, and silent lie?
What booteth then the good and righteous deed,
If goodness find no grace, nor righteousness no meed?

10] If good find grace, and righteousness reward,
Why then is Amoret in captive band,
Since that more bounteous creature never fared
On foot upon the face of living land?
Or if that heavenly justice may withstand
The wrongful outrage of unrighteous men,
Why then is Busirane with wicked hand
Suffered, these se'en-months day, in secret den
My lady and my love so cruelly to pen?

11] My lady and my love is cruelly penned
In doleful darkness from the view of day,
Whilst deadly torments do her chaste breast rend,

7.7 **boy** Cupid   .9 **he** the knight   8.4 **abrade** awaken   9.5
**unwreaked** unavenged   10.2 **caitive** captive   .3 **bounteous**
virtuous   .8 **se'en** seven   **day** time

And the sharp steel doth rive her heart in tway,
All for she Scudamore will not denay.
Yet thou, vile man, vile Scudamore, art sound,
Nor canst her aid, ne canst her foe dismay;
Unworthy wretch to tread upon the ground,
For whom so fair a lady feels so sore a wound!

12]   There a huge heap of singults did oppress
His struggling soul, and swelling throbs empeach
His faltering tongue with pangs of dreariness,
Choking the remnant of his plaintive speech,
As if his days were come to their last reach:
Which when she heard, and saw the ghastly fit
Threat'ning into his life to make a breach,
Both with great ruth and terror she was smit,
Fearing lest from her cage the weary soul would flit.

13]   Tho stooping down she him amovéd light;
Who therewith somewhat starting, up gan look,
And seeing him behind a stranger knight,
Whereas no living creature he mistook,
With great indignance he that sight forsook,
And down again himself disdainfully
Abjecting, th'earth with his fair forehead struck:
Which the bold virgin seeing, gan apply
Fit med'cine to his grief, and spake thus courteously:

14]   Ah, gentle knight, whose keep conceivéd grief
Well seems t'exceed the power of patiénce,
Yet if that heavenly grace some good relief
You send, submit you to high providence,
And ever in your noble heart prepense
That all the sorrow in the world is less
Than virtue's might, and value's confidence,
For who nill bide the burden of distress
Must not here think to live: for life is wretchedness.

---

11.4 **tway** two  .5 **for** because  .6 **yet** now still  12.1 **singults**
sobs  .2 **empeach** impede  13.1 **Tho** then  **amovéd** roused
.3 **him behind** behind him  .4 **whereas . . . mistook** where
he had mistakenly thought there was no living creature  14.5
**prepense** consider  .7 **value's** valor's  .8 **nill** will not

15] Therefore, fair sir, do comfort to you take,
And freely read what wicked felon so
Hath outraged you, and thralled your gentle make.
Perhaps this hand may help to ease your woe,
And wreak your sorrow on your cruel foe:
At least it fair endeavor will apply.
—Those feeling words so near the quick did go,
That up his head he rearéd easily,
And leaning on his elbow, these few words let fly:

16] What boots it plain that cannot be redressed,
And sow vain sorrow in a fruitless ear,
Since power of hand, nor skill of learnéd breast,
Nor worldly price cannot redeem my dear
Out of her thralldom and continual fear?
For he, the tyrant which hath her in ward,
By strong enchantments and black magic lear,
Hath in a dungeon deep her close embarred,
And many dreadful fiends hath 'pointed to her guard.

17] There he tormenteth her most terribly,
And day and night afflicts with mortal pain,
Because to yield him love she doth deny—
Once to me yold, not to be yold again:
But yet by torture he would her constrain
Love to conceive in her disdainful breast;
Till so she do, she must in dole remain,
Nor may by living means be thence released;
What boots it then to plain, that cannot be redressed?

18] With this sad 'hearsal of his heavy stress,
The warlike damsel was empassioned sore,
And said: Sir knight, your cause is nothing less
Than is your sorrow, certes, if not more;
For nothing so much pity doth implore
As gentle lady's helpless misery.

15.2 **read** tell   .3 **make** mate   16.1 **What . . . that** what use
is it to complain about that which   .2 **fruitless** i.e., ear of one
who cannot help   .7 **lear** lore   17.4 **yold** yielded   18.1 **'hersal**
rehearsal   **stress** distress

But yet, if please ye listen to my lore,
I will with proof of last extremity,
Deliver her from thence, or with her for you die.

19] Ah, gentlest knight alive (said Scudamore),
What huge heroic magnanimity
Dwells in thy bounteous breast? What could'st thou more
If she were thine, and thou as now am I?
O spare thy happy days, and them apply
To better boot, but let me die, that ought;
More is more loss: one is enough to die.—
Life is not lost (said she) for which is bought
Endless renown, that more than death is to be sought.

20] Thus she at length persuaded him to rise
And with her wend, to see what new success
Mote him befall upon new enterprise;
His arms, which he had vowed to disprofess,
She gathered up and did about him dress,
And his forwandered steed unto him got:
So forth they both yfere make their progress,
And march not past the mountenance of a shot,
Till they arrived whereas their purpose they did plot.

21] There they, dismounting, drew their weapons bold
And stoutly came unto the castle gate:
Whereas no gate they found them to withhold,
Nor ward to wait at morn and evening late,
But in the porch, that did them sore amate,
A flaming fire, ymixed with smouldery smoke
And stinking sulfur, that with grisly hate
And dreadful horror did all entrance choke,
Enforcéd them their forward footing to revoke.

22] Greatly thereat was Britomart dismayed,
Ne in that stound wist how herself to bear;

.8 **will . . . extremity** undergoing the extreme test   19.6 **boot**
profit   20.6 **forwandered** strayed   .7 **yfere** together   .8 **moun-
tenance** space   21.5 **amate** dismay   22.2 **stound** trouble
**bear** conduct

For danger vain it were to have assayed
That cruel element which all things fear,
Ne none can suffer to approachen near:
And turning back to Scudamore, thus said:
What monstrous enmity provoke we here,
Foolhardy as th'earth's children, the which made
Battle against the gods, so we a god invade?

23]   Danger without discretion to attempt,
Inglorious and beastlike is: therefore, sir knight,
Aread what course of you is safest dempt,
And how we with our foe may come to fight.
This is (quoth he) the dolorous despite
Which erst to you I plained: for neither may
This fire be quenched by any wit or might,
Ne yet by any means removed away,
So mighty be th'enchantments which the same do stay.

24]   What is there else but cease these fruitless pains,
And leave me to my former languishing?
Fair Amoret must dwell in wicked chains,
And Scudamore here die with sorrowing.—
Perdie not so (said she); for shameful thing
It were t'abandon noble chevisance
For show of peril, without venturing:
Rather let try extremities of chance,
Than enterprisèd praise for dread to disadvance.

25]   Therewith resolved to prove her utmost might,
Her ample shield she threw before her face,
And her sword's point directing forward right,
Assailed the flame, the which eftsoons gave place,
And did itself divide with equal space,
That through she passèd, as a thunder bolt
Pierceth the yielding air, and doth displace
The soaring clouds, into sad showers ymolt;
So to her yold the flames, and did their force revolt.

23.3 **Aread** advise   **dempt** deemed, thought   .9 **stay** support
24.5 **Perdie** by heaven   .6 **chevisance** enterprise   .9 **praise**
effort undertaken to gain fame   25.8 **ymolt** melted   .9 **revolt**
turn back

26]  Whom whenas Scudamore saw past the fire,
    Safe and untouched, he likewise gan assay,
    With greedy will and envious desire,
    And bade the stubborn flames to yield him way:
    But cruel Mulciber would not obey
    His threatful pride, but did the more augment
    His mighty rage, and with imperious sway
    Him forced, maugré, his fierceness to relent,
    And back retire, all scorched and pitifully brent.

27]  With huge impatiénce he inly swelt,
    More for great sorrow that he could not pass
    Than for the burning torment which he felt,
    That with fell wodeness he efiercéd was
    And wilfully him throwing on the grass,
    Did beat and bounce his head and breast full sore;
    The whiles the championess now entered has
    The utmost room, and passed the foremost door:
    The utmost room, abounding with all precious store.

28]  For round about, the walls yclothéd were
    With goodly arras of great majesty,
    Woven with gold and silk so close and near
    That the rich metal lurkéd privily,
    As faining to be hid from envious eye;
    Yet here and there, and everywhere unwares
    It showed itself, and shone unwillingly;
    Like a discolored snake, whose hidden snares
    Through the green grass his long bright burnished back de-
        clares.

29]  And in those tapets weren fashionéd
    Many fair portraits, and many a fair feat,
    And all of love, and all of lustihead,
    As seeméd by their semblant, did entreat;
    And eke all Cupid's wars they did repeat,

---

26.5 **Mulciber** god of fire  .9 **brent** burnt  27.1 **swelt** seethed
.4 **wodeness** madness **efierced** maddened  .8 **utmost** outer-
most  28.8 **discolored** multicolored  29.1 **tapets** tapestries  .4
**entreat** treat

And cruel battles which he whilom fought
'Gainst all the gods, to make his empire great;
Besides the huge massacres, which he wrought
On mighty kings and kaisers, into thralldom brought.

30]   Therein was writ, how often thundering Jove
Had felt the point of his heart-piercing dart,
And leaving heaven's kingdom, here did rove
In strange disguise, to slake his scalding smart;
Now like a ram, fair Helle to pervart,
Now like a bull, Europa to withdraw:
Ah, how the fearful lady's tender heart
Did lively seem to tremble, when she saw
The huge seas under her t'obey her servant's law.

31]   Soon after that into a golden shower
Himself he changed fair Danaë to view,
And through the roof of her strong brazen tower
Did rain into her lap an honey dew,
The whiles her foolish guard, that little knew
Of such deceit, kept th'iron door fast barred,
And watched that none should enter or issue;
Vain was the watch, and bootless all the ward,
Whenas the god to golden hue himself transferred.

32]   Then was he turned into a snowy swan,
To win fair Leda to his lovely trade:
O wondrous skill, and sweet wit of the man,
That her in daffodillies sleeping made,
From scorching heat her dainty limbs to shade:
Whiles the proud bird, ruffing his feathers wide,
And brushing his fair breast, did her invade;
She slept, yet 'twixt her eyelids closely spied,
How towards her he rushed, and smiled at his pride.

33]   Then showed it how the Theban Semele,
Deceived of jealous Juno, did require
To see him in his sovereign majesty,

---

.9 **kaisers** emperors   30.5 **pervart** lead away   .8 **lively** lifelike
32.2 **lovely** amorous   .7 **brushing** bristling

Armed with his thunderbolts and lightening fire,
Whence dearly she with death bought her desire.
But fair Alcmene better match did make,
'Joying his love in likeness more entire;
Three nights in one, they say, that for her sake
He then did put, her pleasures longer to partake.

34]  Twice was he seen in soaring eagle's shape,
And with wide wings to beat the buxom air:
Once when he with Asteria did 'scape,
Again whenas the Trojan boy so fair
He snatched from Ida hill, and with him bare:
Wondrous delight it was, there to behold
How the rude shepherds after him did stare,
Trembling through fear lest down he fallen should,
And often to him calling to take surer hold.

35]  In satyr's shape Antiope he snatched;
And like a fire, when he Aegin' assayed;
A shepherd, when Mnemosyne he catched;
And like a serpent to the Thracian maid.
Whiles thus on earth great Jove these pageants played,
The wingéd boy did thrust into his throne,
And, scoffing, thus unto his mother said:
Lo now the heavens obey to me alone,
And take me for their Jove, whiles Jove to earth is gone.

36]  And thou, fair Phoebus, in thy colors bright,
Wast there enwoven, and the sad distress,
In which that boy thee plungéd, for despite
That thou bewray'dst his mother's wantonness,
When she with Mars was meint in joyfulness;
For-thy he thrilled thee with a leaden dart,
To love fair Daphne which thee lovéd less;
Less she thee loved than was thy just desert,
Yet was thy love her death, and her death was thy smart.

33.7 **'Joying** enjoying  34.2 **buxom** yielding  .3 **Asteria** a ti-
taness who turned into a quail to escape Zeus  .3 **boy** Gany-
mede  35.4 **maid** Proserpina  36.5 **meint** mingled  .6 **For-thy**
therefore  **thrilled** pierced

37]  So lovedst thou the lusty Hyacinth;
     So lovedst thou the fair Coronis dear:
     Yet both are of thy hapless hand extinct—
     Yet both in flowers do live, and love thee bear,
     The one a panse, the other a sweet briar:
     For grief whereof, ye mote have lively seen
     The god himself rending his golden hair,
     And breaking quite his garland ever green,
     With other signs of sorrow and impatient teen.

38]  Both for these two, and for his own dear son,
     The son of Climené, he did repent,
     Who bold to guide the chariot of the sun,
     Himself in thousand pieces fondly rent,
     And all the world with flashing fire brent;
     So like, that all the walls did seem to flame.
     Yet cruel Cupid, not herewith content,
     Forced him eftsoons to follow other game,
     And love a shepherd's daughter for his dearest dame.

39]  He lovéd Isse for his dearest dame,
     And for her sake her cattle fed a while—
     And for her sake a cowherd vile became,
     The servant of Admetus, coward vile,
     Whiles that from heaven he sufferéd exile.
     Long were to tell each other lovely fit—
     Now like a lion, hunting after spoil,
     Now like a stag, now like a falcon flit:
     All which in that fair arras was most lively writ.

40]  Next unto him was Neptune picturéd,
     In his divine resemblance wondrous like:
     His face was rugged, and his hoary head
     Droppéd with brackish dew; his three-forked pike
     He sternly shook, and therewith fierce did strike
     The raging billows, that on every side

37.1 **lusty** handsome  .3 **extinct** killed  .5 **panse** pansy  .9
**teen** grief  38.1 **son** Phaeton  .4 **fondly** foolishly  39.4 **cow-
ard** original text spells coward and cowherd the same way  .8
**flit** fleet

They trembling stood, and made a long broad dike,
That his swift chariot might have passage wide,
Which four great hippodames did draw in teamwise tide.

41]   His sea-horses did seem to snort amain,
And from their nostrils blow the briny stream,
That made the sparkling waves to smoke again
And flame with gold, but the white foamy cream
Did shine with silver, and shoot forth his beam.
The god himself did pensive seem and sad,
And hung adown his head, as he did dream:
For privy love his breast empiercéd had,
Ne aught but dear Bisaltis aye could make him glad.

42]   He lovéd eke Iphimedia dear,
And Aeolus' fair daughter, Arne hight,
For whom he turned himself into a steer,
And fed on fodder to beguile her sight.
Also, to win Deucalion's daughter bright,
He turned himself into a dolphin fair.
And like a winged horse he took his flight
To snaky-lock Medusa to repair,
On whom he got fair Pegasus, that flitteth in the air.

43]   Next Saturn was (but who would ever ween
That sullen Saturn ever weened to love?
Yet love is sullen, and Saturnlike seen,
As he did for Erigone it prove),
That to a centaur did himself transmove.
So proved it eke that gracious god of wine,
When for to compass Philyra's hard love,
He turned himself into a fruitful vine,
And into her fair bosom made his grapes decline.

44]   Long were to tell the amorous assays
And gentle pangs, with which he makéd meek
The mighty Mars, to learn his wanton plays:

40.9 **hippodames** sea horses  .9 **teamwise tide** concerted
rhythm  41.8 **privy** secret  42.2 **hight** named  43.1 **ween**
think  .3 **Saturnlike** saturnine  .4 **prove** show, demonstrate
44.2 **he** Cupid

How oft for Venus, and how often eke
For many other nymphs, he sore did shriek,
With womanish tears, and with unwarlike smarts
Privily moistening his horrid cheek.
There was he painted full of burning darts,
And many wide wounds launchéd through his inner parts.

45]   Ne did he spare (so cruel was the elf)
His own dear mother (ah why should he so?);
Ne did he spare sometime to prick himself,
That he might taste the sweet consuming woe
Which he had wrought to many others moe.
But to declare the mournful tragedies
And spoils, wherewith he all the ground did strow:
More eath to number, with how many eyes
High heaven beholds sad lovers' nightly thieveries.

46]   Kings, queens, lords, ladies, knights, and damsels gent
Were heaped together with the vulgar sort,
And mingled with the rascal rabblement,
Without respect of person or of port,
To show Dan Cupid's power and great effort:
And round about a border was entrailed,
Of broken bows and arrows shivered short,
And a long bloody river through them railed,
So lively and so like that living sense it failed.

47]   And at the upper end of that fair room,
There was an altar built of precious stone,
Of passing value, and of great renown,
On which there stood an image all alone,
Of massy gold, which with his own light shone;
And wings it had, with sundry colors dight:
More sundry colors than the proud pavone
Bears in his boasted fan, or Iris bright,
When her discolored bow she spreads through heaven
     bright.

---

.7 **horrid** rough   45.5 **moe** more   .7 **strow** strew   .8 **eath**
easy (it would be easier . . . )   46.4 **port** importance   .5 **Dan**
lord   .8 **railed** flowed   .9 **failed** misled   47.7 **pavone** pea-
cock

48]  Blindfold he was, and in his cruel fist
      A mortal bow and arrows keen did hold,
      With which he shot at random, when him list:
      Some headed with sad lead, some with pure gold
      (Ah man beware, how thou those darts behold).
      A wounded dragon under him did lie,
      Whose hideous tail his left foot did enfold,
      And with a shaft was shot though either eye,
      That no man forth might draw, nor no man remedy.

49]  And underneath his feet was written thus:
      *Unto the Victor of the Gods this be;*
      And all the people in that ample house
      Did to that image bow their humble knee,
      And oft committed foul idolatry.
      That wondrous sight fair Britomart amazed,
      Ne seeing could her wonder satisfy,
      But ever more and more upon it gazed,
      The whiles the passing brightness her frail senses dazed.

50]  Tho as she backward cast her busy eye
      To search each secret of that goodly stead,
      Over the door thus written she did spy
      *Be bold.* She oft and oft it over read,
      Yet could not find what sense it figuréd:
      But what so were therein or writ or meant,
      She was no whit thereby discouragéd
      From prosecuting of her first intent,
      But forward with bold steps into the next room went.

51]  Much fairer than the former was that room,
      And richlier by many parts arrayed:
      For not with arras made in painful loom,
      But with pure gold it all was overlaid,
      Wrought with wild antics, which their follies played
      In the rich metal as they living were:
      A thousand monstrous forms therein were made,

48.3 **him list** he wished  49.9 **passing** surpassing  50.2 **stead** place  .6 **or** either  51.3 **painful** painstaking  .5 **antics** fantastic figures

Such as false love doth oft upon him wear,
For love in thousand monstrous forms doth oft appear.

52]   And, all about, the glistering walls were hung
With warlike spoils, and with victorious preys
Of mighty conquerors and captains strong,
Which were whilom captivéd in their days
To cruel love, and wrought their own decays:
Their swords and spears were broke, and hauberks rent;
And their proud garlands of triumphant bays
Trodden in dust with fury insolent,
To show the victor's might and merciless intent.

53]   The warlike maid beholding earnestly
The goodly ordinance of this rich place,
Did greatly wonder, ne could satisfy
Her greedy eyes with gazing a long space,
But more she marvelled that no footing's trace
Nor wight appeared, but wasteful emptiness,
And solemn silence over all that place:
Strange thing it seemed, that none was to possess
So rich purveyance, ne them keep with carefulness.

54]   And, as she looked about, she did behold
How over that same door was likewise writ,
*Be bold, be bold*, and everywhere *Be bold*;
That much she mused, yet could not construe it
By any riddling skill, or common wit.
At last she spied at that room's upper end,
Another iron door, on which was writ,
*Be not too bold*. Whereto though she did bend
Her earnest mind, yet wist not what it might intend.

55]   Thus she there waited until eventide,
Yet living creature none she saw appear:
And now sad shadows gan the world to hide
From mortal view, and wrap in darkness drear;
Yet nould she doff her weary arms, for fear
Of secret danger, ne let sleep oppress

52.7 **bays** laurel   53.6 **wasteful** desolate   .8 **was** was there
55.5 **nould** would not

Her heavy eyes with Nature's burden dear,
But drew herself aside in sikerness,
And her well 'pointed weapons did about her dress.


## Canto xii

1 ] Tho whenas cheerless night ycovered had
Fair heaven with an universal cloud,
That every wight, dismayed with darkness sad,
In silence and in sleep themselves did shroud,
She heard a shrilling trumpet sound aloud—
Sign of nigh battle, or got victory—
Naught therewith daunted was her courage proud,
But rather stirred to cruel enmity,
Expecting ever, when some foe she might descry.

2] With that, an hideous storm of wind arose,
With dreadful thunder and lightening atwixt,
And an earthquake, as if it straight would loose
The world's foundations from his center fixed;
A direful stench of smoke and sulfur mixed
Ensued, whose noyance filled the fearful stead,
From the fourth hour of night until the sixth;
Yet the bold Britoness was naught ydread,
Though much enmoved, but steadfast still persévéréd.

3] All suddenly a stormy whirlwind blew
Throughout the house, that clappéd every door,
With which that iron wicket open flew,
As it with mighty levers had been tore:
And forth issued, as on the ready floor
Of some theatre, a grave personage,
That in his hand a branch of laurel bore,
With comely 'haviór and count'nance sage,
Yclad in costly garments, fit for tragic stage.

.8 **silkerness** sureness, safety 1.9 **Expecting** awaiting 2.2
**atwixt** mixed .4 **center fixed** fixed center .7 **sixth** there were
twelve hours of darkness

4] Proceeding to the midst, he still did stand,
　　As if in mind he somewhat had to say;
　　And to the vulgar beckoning with his hand,
　　In sign of silence, as to hear a play,
　　By lively actións he gan bewray
　　Some argument of matter passionéd;
　　Which done, he back retiréd soft away,
　　And passing by, his name discoveréd:
　　*Ease*, on his robe in golden letters cipheréd.


5] The noble maid, still standing, all this viewed,
　　And marvelled at his strange intendiment;
　　With that a joyous fellowship issued
　　Of minstrels, making goodly merriment,
　　With wanton bards, and rhymers impudent,
　　All which together sung full cheerfully
　　A lay of love's delight, with sweet consent:
　　After whom marched a jolly company,
　　In manner of a masque, enrangéd orderly.


6] The whiles a most delicious harmony
　　In full strange notes was sweetly heard to sound,
　　That the rare sweetness of the melody
　　The feeble senses wholly did confound,
　　And the frail soul in deep delight nigh drowned:
　　And when it ceased, shrill trumpets loud did bray,
　　That their report did far away rebound,
　　And when they ceased, it gan again to play,
　　The whiles the maskers marchéd forth in trim array.


7] The first was Fancy, like a lovely boy,
　　Of rare aspect and beauty without peer;
　　Matchable either to that imp of Troy
　　Whom Jove did love, and chose his cup to bear,
　　Or that same dainty lad which was so dear

---

4.3 **the vulgar** the crowd　5.2 **intendiment** intention　.7 **consent** harmony　7.3 **imp** offshoot, i.e., Ganymede

To great Alcides, that, whenas he died,
He wailéd womanlike with many a tear,
And every wood, and every valley wide
He filled with Hylas' name; the nymphs eke "Hylas" cried.

8] His garment neither was of silk nor say,
But painted plumes, in goodly order dight,
Like as the sunburnt Indians do array
Their tawny bodies, in their proudest plight:
As those same plumes, so seemed he vain and light,
That by his gait might easily appear;
For still he fared as dancing in delight,
And in his hand a windy fan did bear,
That, in the idle air, he moved still here and there.

9] And him beside marched amorous Desire,
Who seemed of riper years than th'other swain:
Yet was that other swain this elder's sire,
And gave him being, common to them twain;
His garment was disguiséd very vain,
And his embroidered bonnet sat awry;
Twixt both his hands few sparks he close did strain,
Which still he blew and kindled busily,
That soon they life conceived, and forth in flames did fly.

10] Next after him went Doubt, who was yclad
In a discolored coat of strange disguise,
That at his back a broad capuccio had,
And sleeves dependent Albanesé-wise;
He looked askew with his mistrustful eyes,
And nicely trod, as thorns lay in his way
Or that the floor to shrink he did avise,
And on a broken reed he still did stay
His feeble steps, which shrunk when hard thereon he lay.

---

.6 **Alcides** Hercules   8.1 **say** fine wool   .2 **painted** colored
.4 **plight** attire   .7 **still** continually   9.5 **disguised** oddly
fashioned   .7 **few . . . strain** he tightly held a few sparks   10.2
**disguise** fashion   .3 **capuccio** hood   .4 **dependent Albanese-wise** hanging down in Albanian (?) fashion   .6 **nicely** carefully
.7 **avise** suppose

11]  With him went Danger, clothed in ragged weed
     Made of bear's skin, that him more dreadful made;
     Yet his own face was dreadful, nor did need
     Strange horror to deform his grisly shade;
     A net in th'one hand, and a rusty blade
     In th'other was: this Mischief, that Mishap;
     With th'one his foes he threatened to invade,
     With th'other he his friends meant to enwrap:
     For, whom he could not kill, he practiced to entrap.

12]  Next him was Fear, all armed from top to toe,
     Yet thought himself not safe enough thereby,
     But feared each shadow moving to and fro,
     And his own arms when glittering he did spy,
     Or clashing heard, he fast away did fly,
     As ashes pale of hue, and wingy-heeled;
     And evermore on Danger fixed his eye,
     'Gainst whom he always bent a brazen shield,
     Which his right hand unarmèd fearfully did wield.

13]  With him went Hope in rank, a handsome maid
     Of cheerful look and lovely to behold;
     In silken samite she was light arrayed,
     And her fair locks were woven up in gold;
     She alway smiled, and in her hand did hold
     An holy water sprinkle, dipped in dew,
     With which she sprinkled favors manifold
     On whom she list, and did great liking show:
     Great liking unto many, but true love to few.

14]  And after them Dissemblance and Suspect
     Marched in one rank, yet an unequal pair:
     For she was gentle and of mild aspect,
     Courteous to all and seeming debonair,
     Goodly adornèd and exceeding fair:
     Yet was that all but painted and purloined,

---

11.1 **weed** garment   .4 **Strange** other   **shade** coloring, ghostly
appearance   13.1 **in rank** side by side   14.1 **Suspect** suspicion

And her bright brows were decked with borrowed hair:
Her deeds were forgéd, and her words false coined,
And always in her hand two clews of silk she twined.

15] But he was foul, ill favoréd, and grim,
Under his eyebrows looking still askance;
And ever as Dissemblance laughed on him,
He lowered on her with dangerous eye-glance,
Showing his nature in his countenance,
His rolling eyes did never rest in place,
But walked each where, for fear of hid mischance,
Holding a lattice still before his face,
Through which he still did peep, as forward he did pace.

16] Next him went Grief and Fury, matched yfere;
Grief all in sable sorrowfully clad,
Down-hanging his dull head, with heavy cheer,
Yet inly being more than seeming sad:
A pair of pincers in his hand he had,
With which he pinchéd people to the heart,
That from thenceforth a wretched life they led,
In wilful languor and consuming smart,
Dying each day with inward wounds of dolor's dart.

17] But Fury was full ill appareléd
In rags, that naked nigh she did appear,
With ghastly looks and dreadful drearihead;
For from her back her garments she did tear,
And from her head oft rent her snarléd hair;
In her right hand a firebrand she did toss
About her head, still roaming here and there:
As a dismayéd deer, in chase embossed,
Forgetful of his safety, hath his right way lost.

18] After them went Displeasure and Pleasance—
He looking lumpish and full sullen sad
And hanging down his heavy countenance;

.9 **clews** balls of thread, to lead through a labyrinth; i.e., she
mixes up the clues   15.8 **lattice** a screen to spy through   17.3
**-head** -ness   .8 **embossed** hard pressed

She cheerful fresh and full of joyance glad,
As if no sorrow she ne felt ne drad—
That evil matchéd pair they seemed to be:
An angry wasp th'one in a vial had,
Th'other in hers a honey-laden bee;
Thus marchéd these six couples forth in fair degree.

19] After all these there marched a most fair dame,
Led of two grisly villains, th'one Despite,
The other clepéd Cruelty by name:
She, doleful lady, like a dreary spright,
Called by strong charms out of eternal night,
Had death's own image figured in her face,
Full of sad signs, fearful to living sight;
Yet in that horror showed a seemly grace,
And with her feeble feet did move a comely pace.

20] Her breast—all naked, as net ivory,
Without adorn of gold or silver bright,
Wherewith the craftsman wonts it beautify—
Of her due honor was despoiléd quite,
And a wide wound therein (O rueful sight)
Entrenchéd deep with knife accurséd keen,
Yet freshly bleeding forth her fainting spright,
(The work of cruel hand) was to be seen,
That dyed in sanguine red her skin all snowy clean.

21] At that wide orifice her trembling heart
Was drawn forth, and in silver basin laid,
Quite through transfixéd with a deadly dart,
And in her blood yet steaming fresh embayed:
And those two villains which her steps upstayed,
When her weak feet could scarcely her sustain
And fading vital powers gan to fade,
Her forward still with torture did constrain,
And evermore increaséd her consuming pain.

22] Next after her the wingéd god himself
Came riding on a lion ravenous,

18.9 **degree** rank   19.3 **clepéd** called   .4 **spright** spirit   20.1
**net** pure, neat   .4 **honor** adornment   21.4 **embayed** bathed

Taught to obey the manage of that elf
That man and beast with power imperious
Subdueth to his kingdom tyrannous:
His blindfold eyes he bade a while unbind,
That his proud spoil of that same dolorous
Fair dame he might behold in perfect kind;
Which seen, he much rejoicéd in his cruel mind.

23] Of which full proud, himself up rearing high,
He lookéd round about with stern disdain,
And did survey his goodly company;
And marshalling the evil ordered train:
With that, the darts which his right hand did strain,
Full dreadfully he shook, that all did quake,
And clapped on high his colored wingés twain,
That all his meny it afraid did make:
Tho, blinding him again, his way he forth did take.

24] Behind him was Reproach, Repentance, Shame:
Reproach the first, Shame next, Repent behind;
Repentance feeble, sorrowful, and lame;
Reproach despiteful, careless, and unkind;
Shame most ill favored, bestial, and blind:
Shame lowered, Repentance sighed, Reproach did scold;
Reproach sharp stings, Repentance whips entwined,
Shame burning brand-irons in her hand did hold:
All three to each unlike, yet all made in one mold.

25] And after them a rude confuséd rout
Of persons flocked, whose names is hard to read:
Amongst them was stern Strife, and Anger stout;
Unquiet Care, and fond Unthriftihead,
Lewd Loss of Time, and Sorrow, seeming dead,
Inconstant Change, and false Disloyalty;
Consuming Riotise, and guilty Dread
Of heavenly vengeance; faint Infirmity,
Vile Poverty, and lastly Death-with-Infamy.

22.8 **in perfect kind** perfectly    23.8 **meny** followers    24.9 **each** each other    25.2 **read** determine    .7 **Riotise** dissolute living

26]   There were full many more like maladies,
    Whose names and natures I no'te readen well;
    So many more as there be fantasies
    In wavering women's wit, that none can tell,
    Or pains in love, or punishments in hell;
    All which disguiséd marched in masking wise
    About the chamber with that damosel,
    And then returnéd, having marchéd thrice,
Into the inner room, from whence they first did rise.

27]   So soon as they were in, the door straightway
    Fast lockéd, driven with that stormy blast
    Which first it opened, and bore all away.
    Then the brave maid, which all this while was placed
    In secret shade, and saw both first and last,
    Issued forth, and went unto the door
    To enter in, but found it lockéd fast:
    It vain she thought with rigorous uproar
For to efforce, when charms had closéd it afore.

28]   Where force might not avail, there sleights and art
    She cast to use, both fit for hard emprize;
    For-thy from that same room not to depart
    Till morrow next, she did herself avise,
    When that same masque again should forth arise.
    The morrow next appeared with joyous cheer,
    Calling men to their daily exercise;
    Then she, as morrow fresh, herself did rear
Out of her secret stand, that day for to outwear.

29]   All that day she outwore in wandering
    And gazing on that chamber's ornament,
    Till that again the second evening
    Her covered with her sable vestiment,
    Wherewith the world's fair beauty she hath blent;
    Then when the second watch was almost past,

26.2 **no'te** do not know how to   28.2 **emprize** enterprise   .4
**herself avise** resolve   .6 **morrow** morning   29.5 **blent** ob-
scured   .6 **when . . . past** midnight, second of the night's four
watches

That brazen door flew open, and in went
Bold Britomart, as she had late forecast,
Neither of idle shows nor of false charms aghast.

30] So soon as she was entered, round about
She cast her eyes, to see what was become
Of all those persons, which she saw without:
But lo, they straight were vanished, all and some,
Ne living wight she saw in all that room,
Save that same woeful lady, both whose hands
Were bounden fast, that did her ill become,
And her small waist girt round with iron bands
Unto a brazen pillar, by the which she stands.

31] And her before the vile enchanter sat,
Figuring strange characters of his art;
With living blood he those characters wrote,
Dreadfully dropping from her dying heart,
Seeming transfixéd with a cruel dart—
And all perforce to make her him to love.
Ah, who can love the worker of her smart?
A thousand charms he formerly did prove;
Yet thousand charms could not her steadfast heart remove.

32] Soon as that virgin knight he saw in place,
His wicked books in haste he overthrew,
Not caring his long labors to deface;
And fiercely running to that lady true,
A murderous knife out of his pocket drew,
The which he thought, for villainous despite,
In her tormented body to imbrue:
But the stout damsel, to him leaping light,
His ccurséd hand withheld, and masteréd his might.

31.1 **her before** before her .2 **Figuring strange characters**
writing strange inscriptions .8 **prove** try 32.2 **his . . . deface**
that he ruined his long labors .4 **lady true** Amoret .8 **damsel**
Britomart

33]  From her to whom his fury first he meant,
     The wicked weapon rashly he did wrest,
     And turning to herself his fell intent,
     Unwares it struck into her snowy chest,
     That little drops empurpled her fair breast.
     Exceeding wroth therewith the virgin grew—
     Albe the wound were nothing deep impressed—
     And fiercely forth her mortal blade she drew,
     To give him the reward for such vile outrage due.

34]  So mightily she smote him that to ground
     He fell half dead: next stroke him should have slain,
     Had not the lady, which by him stood bound,
     Dernly unto her callèd to abstain
     From doing him to die. For else her pain
     Should be remediless, since none but he
     Which wrought it could the same recure again.
     Therewith she stayed her hand, loath stayed to be;
     For life she him envied, and longed revenge to see.

35]  And to him said: Thou wicked man, whose meed
     For so huge mischief and vile villainy
     Is death, or if that aught to death exceed—
     Be sure that naught may save thee from to die,
     But if that thou this dame do presently
     Restore unto her health and former state;
     This do and live, else die undoubtedly.
     He, glad of life, that looked for death but late,
     Did yield himself right willing to prolong his date.

36]  And rising up, gan straight to overlook
     Those cursed leaves, his charms back to reverse;
     Full dreadful things out of that baleful book
     He read, and measured many a sad verse,
     That horror gan the virgin's heart to pierce,
     And her fair locks up starèd stiff on end,
     Hearing him those same bloody lines rehearse;

33.2 **rashly . . . wrest** he quickly swerved (to direct it against
Britomart)  .7 **Albe** although  34.4 **Dernly** dismally  .9 **en-
vied** begrudged  35.3 **or . . . exceed** or worse, if there is any-
thing worse  .5 **But if** unless  .9 **date** end  36.1 **straight to
overlook** immediately look through

And all the while he read, she did extend
Her sword high over him, if aught he did offend.

37] Anon she gan perceive the house to quake,
And all the doors to rattle round about;
Yet all that did not her dismayéd make,
Nor slack her threatful hand for danger's doubt,
But still with steadfast eye and courage stout
Abode, to weet what end would come of all.
At last that mighty chain, which round about
Her tender waist was wound, adown gan fall,
And that great brazen pillar broke in pieces small.

38] The cruel steel which thrilled her dying heart
Fell softly forth, as of his own accord:
And the wide wound, which lately did dispart
Her bleeding breast, and riven bowels gored,
Was closéd up, as it had not been bored:
And every part to saféty full sound,
As she were never hurt, was soon restored;
Tho when she felt herself to be unbound,
And perfect whole, prostrate she fell unto the ground:

39] Before Fair Britomart she fell prostrate,
Saying: Ah noble knight, what worthy meed
Can wretched lady, quit from woeful state,
Yield you in lieu of this your gracious deed?
Your virtue self her own reward shall breed—
Even immortal praise and glory wide,
Which I your vassal, by your prowess freed,
Shall through the world make to be notified,
And goodly well advance that goodly well was tried.

40] But Britomart uprearing her from ground,
Said: Gentle dame, reward enough I ween
For many labors more than I have found,
This, that in safety now I have you seen,
And means of your deliverance have been;

.9 **if aught** lest in any way   37.6 **weet** know   .8 **her** Amoret's
38.1 **thrilled** pierced   .3 **dispart** cleave   39.3 **quit** released
.9 **advance . . . tried** praise that which was well tested

Henceforth, fair lady, comfort to you take,
And put away remembrance of late teen;
Instead thereof, know that your loving make
Hath no less grief enduréd for your gentle sake.

41]   She much was cheered to hear him mentionéd
Whom of all living wights she lovéd best.
Then laid the noble championess strong hand
Upon th'enchanter, which had her distressed
So sore, and with foul outrages oppressed:
With that great chain, wherewith not long ago
He bound that piteous lady prisoner, now released,
Himself she bound (more worthy to be so),
And captive with her led to wretchedness and woe.

42]   Returning back, those goodly rooms which erst
She saw so rich and royally arrayed,
Now vanished utterly and clean subversed
She found, and all their glory quite decayed,
That sight of such a change her much dismayed.
Thenceforth descending to that per'lous porch,
Those dreadful flames she also found delayed,
And quenchéd quite, like a consuméd torch,
That erst all enterers wont so cruelly to scorch.

43]   More easy issue now than entrance late
She found: for now that feignéd dreadful flame
Which choked the porch of that enchanted gate,
And passage barred to all that thither came,
Was vanished quite, as it were not the same,
And gave her leave at pleasure forth to pass.
Th'enchanter self, which all that fraud did frame,
To have efforced the love of that fair lass,
Seeing his work now wasted deep engrievéd was.

44]   But when the victoress arrivéd there
Where late she left the pensive Scudamore,

41.7 **He . . . released** a hexameter line   42.7 **delayed**   put out
43.2 **feignéd**   false

With her own trusty squire, both full of fear,
Neither of them she found where she them lore:
Thereat her noble heart was 'stonished sore;
But most fair Amoret, whose gentle spright
Now gan to feed on hope (which she before
Conceivéd had) to see her own dear knight,
Being thereof beguiled, was filled with new affright.

45]  But he, sad man, when he had long in dread
Awaited there for Britomart's return,
Yet saw her not nor sign of her good speed,
His expectation to despair did turn,
Misdeeming sure that her those flames did burn;
And therefore gan advise with her old squire
(Who her dear nurseling's loss no less did mourn)
Thence to depart for further aid t'inquire:
Where let them wend at will, whilst here I do respire.

44.4 **lore** left   .9 **beguiled** cheated   45.3 **good speed** success
.5 **Misdeeming** wrongly thinking   .6 **squire** i.e., her nurse   .9
**respire** take breath, pause

# Book IV

## Canto i

1] Of lovers' sad calamities of old
   Full many piteous stories do remain,
   But none more piteous ever was ytold
   Than that of Amoret's heart-binding chain,
   And this of Florimel's unworthy pain:
   The dear compassion of whose bitter fit
   My softened heart so sorely doth constrain,
   That I with tears full oft do pity it
   And oftentimes do wish it never had been writ.

2] For from the time that Scudamore her bought
   In perilous fight, she never joyéd day:
   A perilous fight when he with force her brought
   From twenty knights, that did him all assay;
   Yet fairly well he did them all dismay,
   And with great glory both the shield of love
   And eke the lady self he brought away—
   Whom, having wedded as did him behoove,
   A new unknowen mischief did from him remove.

3] For that same vile enchanter Busirane,
   The very self same day that she was wedded,
   Amidst the bridal feast, whilst every man,
   Surcharged with wine, were heedless and ill headed,
   All bent to mirth before the bride was bedded,
   Brought in that masque of love which late was shown:
   And there the lady, ill of friends besteaded

1.5 **unworthy** undeserved (Florimel is another lady in distress;
her story is told alternately with Amoret's) .6 **dear compassion
of** great compassion for 2.1 **her bought** gained Amoret .3
**fight** narrated in IV, below

116

(By way of sport, as oft in masques is known),
Conveyéd quite away, to living wight unknown.

4] Seven months he so her kept in bitter smart,
Because his sinful lust she would not serve;
Until such time as noble Britomart
Releaséd her, that else was like to sterve,
Through cruel knife that her dear heart did carve.
And now she is with her upon the way,
Marching in lovely wise, that could deserve
No spot of blame, though spite did oft assay
To blot her with dishonor of so fair a prey.

## Canto x

*In the course of Book IV ("Of Friendship"), Scuda-more, who has still not been reunited with Amoret, tells how he wooed and won her. He is the speaker of the following canto.* [Eds.]

1] True he it said (whatever man it said)
That love with gall and honey doth abound,
But if the one be with the other weighed,
For every dram of honey therein found,
A pound of gall doth over it redound.
That I too true by trial have approved:
For since the day that first with deadly wound
My heart was launched, and learnéd to have loved,
I never joyéd hour, but still with care was moved.

2] And yet such grace is given them from above
That all the cares and evil which they meet
May naught at all their settled minds remove,
But seem, 'gainst common sense, to them most sweet,
As boasting in their martyrdom unmeet.
So all that ever yet I have endured,
I count as naught, and tread down under feet,

4.4 **sterve** die  .7 **lovely** affectionate  .9 **prey** prize  1.8
**launched** pierced  .9 **still** always  2.1 **them** lovers  .5 **As
. . . unmeet** as if they boasted of their undeserved martyrdom

Since of my love at length I rest assured,
That to disloyalty she will not be allured.

3] Long were to tell the travail and long toil
Through which this shield of love I late have won,
And purchaséd this peerless beauty's spoil,
That harder may be ended than begun;
But since ye so desire, your will be done.
Then hark ye, gentle knights and ladies free,
My hard mishaps, that ye may learn to shun;
For though sweet love to conquer glorious be,
Yet is the pain thereof much greater than the fee.

4] What time the fame of this renownéd prize
Flew first abroad, and all men's ears possessed,
I having arms then taken, gan avise
To win me honor by some noble gest,
And purchase me some place amongst the best.
I boldly thought (so young men's thoughts are bold)
That this same brave emprize for me did rest,
And that both shield and she whom I behold
Might be my lucky lot—sith all by lot we hold.

5] So on that hard adventure forth I went,
And to the place of peril shortly came.
That was a temple, fair and ancient,
Which of great mother Venus bare the name,
And far renownéd through exceeding fame;
Much more than that which was in Paphos built,
Or that in Cyprus, both long since this same,
Though all the pillars of the one were gilt,
And all the other's pavement were with ivory spilt.

6] And it was seated in an island strong,
Abounding all with delices most rare,
And walled by Nature 'gainst invaders' wrong;
That none mote have access, nor inward fare,

3.3 **purchaséd** won   .4 **that** i.e., the toil   .9 **fee** reward   4.1
**prize** Amoret   .4 **gest** deed   .9 **sith** since   **lot** portion, or
chance   5.9 **split** covered   6.2 **delices** delights

But by one way, that passage did prepare:
It was a bridge ybuilt in goodly wise,
With curious corbs and pendants graven fair,
And, archéd all with porches, did arise
On stately pillars, framed after the Doric guise.

7] And for defence thereof, on th'other end
There rearéd was a castle fair and strong,
That warded all which in or out did wend,
And flankéd both the bridge's sides along
'Gainst all that would it feign to force or wrong.
And therein wonéd twenty valiant knights—
All twenty tried in war's experience long—
Whose office was against all manner wights
By all means to maintain that castle's ancient rights.

8] Before that castle was an open plain,
And in the midst thereof a pillar placed,
On which this shield, of many sought in vain—
The shield of Love, whose guerdon me hath graced—
Was hanged on high, with golden ribbons laced;
And in the marble stone was written this,
With golden letters goodly well enchased:
*Blesséd the man that well can use his bliss:*
*Whose ever be the shield, fair Amoret be his.*

9] Which when I read, my heart did inly yearn
And pant with hope of that adventure's hap:
Nor stayéd further news thereof to learn,
But with my spear upon the shield did rap,
That all the castle ringéd with the clap.
Straight forth issued a knight all armed to proof,
And bravely mounted, to his most mishap:
Who staying naught to question from aloof,
Ran fierce at me, that fire glanced from his horse's hoof;

10] Whom boldly I encountered as I could,
And by good fortune shortly him unseated.

.5 **prepare** provide   .7 **corbs** corbels   7.5 **it . . . force** suppose, imagine to force it   .6 **wonéd** dwelled   9.2 **hap** fortune
.8 **aloof** apart

Eftsoons out sprung two more of equal mold,
But I them both with equal hap defeated;
So all the twenty I likewise entreated,
And left them groaning there upon the plain.
Then pressing to the pillar I repeated
The reed thereof for guerdon of my pain,
And taking down the shield, with me did it retain.

11]   So forth without impediment I passed,
Till to the bridge's utter gate I came:
The which I found sure locked and chainéd fast.
I knocked, but no man answered me by name;
I called, but no man answered to my claim.
Yet I persévered still to knock and call,
Till at the last I spied within the same
Where one stood peeping through a crevice small,
To whom I called aloud, half angry therewithal.

12]   That was, to wit, the porter of the place,
Unto whose trust the charge thereof was lent:
His name was Doubt, that had a double face,
Th'one forward looking, th'other backward bent,
Therein resembling Janus ancient,
Which hath in charge the ingate of the year;
And evermore his eyes about him went,
As if some provéd peril he did fear,
Or did misdoubt some ill, whose cause did not appear.

13]   On th'one side he, on th'other sat Delay—
Behind the gate, that none might her espy—
Whose manner was all passengers to stay,
And entertain with her occasions sly,
Through which some lost great hope unheedily,
Which never they recover might again;
And others, quite excluded forth, did lie
Long languishing there in unpitied pain,
And seeking often entrance afterwards in vain.

10.7–8 **repeated the reed** reconsidered the sense   11.2 **utter**
outer   .5 **claim** clamor   12.6 **ingate** entrance   13.4 **occasions**
pretexts

14] Me whenas he had privily espied,
   Bearing the shield which I had conquered late,
   He kenned it straight, and to me opened wide.
   So in I passed, and straight he closed the gate.
   But being in, Delay in close await
   Caught hold on me, and thought my steps to stay,
   Feigning full many a fond excuse to prate,
   And time to steal, the treasure of man's day,
   Whose smallest minute lost, no riches render may.

15] But by no means my way I would forslow,
   For aught that ever she could do or say;
   But from my lofty steed dismounting low,
   Passed forth on foot, beholding all the way
   The goodly works and stones of rich assay
   Cast into sundry shapes by wondrous skill,
   That like on earth nowhere I reckon may:
   And underneath, the river rolling still
   With murmurs soft, that seemed to serve the workman's
      will.

16] Thence forth I passéd to the second gate,
   The Gate of Good Desert, whose goodly pride
   And costly frame were long here to relate.
   The same to all stood always open wide:
   But in the porch did evermore abide
   A hideous giant, dreadful to behold,
   That stopped the entrance with his spacious stride,
   And with the terror of his countenance bold
   Full many did affray, that else fain enter would.

17] His name was Danger, dreaded over all,
   Who day and night did watch and duly ward,
   From fearful cowards entrance to forstall,
   And faint-heart fools, whom show of peril hard
   Could terrify from Fortune's fair award:
   For oftentimes faint hearts at first espial

14.3 **kenned** recognized  .7 **fond** foolish  15.9 **workman's** the
maker of the bridge's  16.2 **Desert** deserving

Of his grim face were from approaching scared:
Unworthy they of grace, whom one denial
Excludes from fairest hope, withouten further trial.

18] Yet many doughty warriors, often tried
In greater perils to be stout and bold,
Durst not the sternness of his look abide,
But soon as they his countenance did behold,
Began to faint, and feel their courage cold.
Again some other, that in hard assays
Were cowards known, and little count did hold,
Either through gifts or guile, or such like ways,
Crept in by stooping low, or stealing of the keys.

19] But I, though meanest man of many moe,
Yet much disdaining unto him to lout,
Or creep between his legs, so in to go,
Resolved him to assault with manhood stout,
And either beat him in or drive him out.
Eftsoons advancing that enchanted shield,
With all my might I gan to lay about:
Which when he saw, the glaive which he did wield
He gan forthwith t'avale, and way unto me yield.

20] So as I entered, I did backward look,
For fear of harm that might lie hidden there;
And lo, his hindparts, whereof heed I took,
Much more deforméd fearful ugly were
Than all his former parts did erst appear:
For hatred, murder, treason, and despite,
With many moe, lay in ambushment there,
Awaiting to entrap the wareless wight
Which did not them prevent with vigilant foresight.

21] Thus having passed all peril, I was come
Within the compass of that island's space;

18.1 **tried** proved   .5 **cold** cool, turn cold   .7 **little . . . hold**
were thought little of   19.2 **lout** bow down   .9 **t'avale** to
lower   20.8 **wareless** heedless   .9 **prevent** anticipate

The which did seem unto my simple doom
The only pleasant and delightful place
That ever trodden was of footing's trace:
For all that Nature by her mother wit
Could frame in earth, and form of substance base,
Was there, and all that Nature did omit,
Art, playing second Nature's part, supplièd it.

22]   No tree, that is of count, in greenwood grows,
      From lowest juniper to cedar tall,
      No flower in field, that dainty odor throws
      And decks his branch with blossoms over all,
      But there was planted, or grew natural:
      Nor sense of man so coy and curious nice,
      But there might find to please itself withal;
      Nor heart could wish for any quaint device,
      But there it present was, and did frail sense entice.

23]   In such luxurious plenty of all pleasure,
      It seemed a second paradise to guess,
      So lavishly enriched with Nature's treasure
      That if the happy souls which do possess
      Th'Elysian fields, and live in lasting bliss,
      Should happen this with living eye to see,
      They soon would loathe their lesser happiness,
      And wish to life returned again to be,
      That in this joyous place they mote have joyance free.

24]   Fresh shadows, fit to shroud from sunny ray;
      Fair lawns, to take the sun in season due;
      Sweet springs, in which a thousand nymphs did play;
      Soft rumbling brooks, that gentle slumber drew;
      High rearéd mounts, the lands about to view;
      Low looking dales, disloined from common gaze;
      Delightful bowers, to solace lovers true;
      False labyrinths, fond runners' eyes to daze:
      All which by Nature made did Nature self amaze.

21.5 **that . . . trace** where anyone had ever walked   22.1 **count**
account   .6 **coy . . . nice** elaborately fastidious   .8 **quaint device** elegant arrangements   23.2 **to guess** one would think
24.5 **about** roundabout   .6 **disloined** removed

25] And all without were walks and alleys dight
With divers trees, enranged in even ranks;
And here and there were pleasant arbors pight,
And shady seats and sundry flowering banks,
To sit and rest the walker's weary shanks;
And therein thousand pairs of lovers walked,
Praising their god, and yielding him great thanks,
Ne ever aught but of their true loves talked,
Ne ever for rebuke, or blame of any, balked.

26] All these together by themselves did sport
Their spotless pleasures, and sweet love's content.
But far away from these, another sort
Of lovers linkéd in true heart's concent:
Which lovéd not as these, for like intent,
But on chaste virtue grounded their desire,
Far from all fraud or feignéd blandishment;
Which in their spirits kindling zealous fire,
Brave thoughts and noble deeds did evermore aspire.

27] Such were great Hercules and Hylas dear;
True Jonathan and David trusty tried;
Stout Theseus, and Pirithous his fere;
Pylades and Orestes by his side;
Mild Titus and Gesippus without pride;
Damon and Pythias, whom death could not sever;
All these and all that ever had been tied
In bands of friendship, there did live forever,
Whose lives although decayed, yet loves decayéd never.

28] Which, whenas I, that never tasted bliss
Nor happy hour, beheld with gazeful eye,
I thought there was none other heaven than this,
And gan their endless happiness envy,

---

25.3 **pight** arranged   26.4 **concent** harmony   .5 **not . . . intent** not with the same intention as the lovers mentioned before. (The pairs below are friends, without necessarily sexual implication)   27.3 **fere** comrade   .5 **Titus and Gesippus** friends from a tale by Boccaccio

That being free from fear and jealousy
Might frankly there their love's desire possess,
Whilst I, through pains and per'lous jeopardy,
Was forced to seek my life's dear patroness:
Much dearer be the things which come through hard dis-
　　tress.

29]　Yet all those sights, and all that else I saw,
Might not my steps withhold, but that forthright
Unto that purposed place I did me draw,
Whereas my love was lodgéd day and night:
The temple of great Venus, that is hight
The queen of beauty, and of love the mother,
There worshippéd of every living wight;
Whose goodly workmanship far passed all other
That ever were on earth, all were they set together.

30]　Not that same famous temple of Diane,
Whose height all Ephesus did oversee,
And which all Asia sought with vows profane—
One of the world's seven wonders said to be—
Might match with this by many a degree;
Nor that which that wise king of Jewry framed,
With endless cost, to be th'Almighty's see;
Nor all that, else, through all the world is named
To all the heathen gods, might like to this be claimed.

31]　I much admiring that so goodly frame,
Unto the porch approached, which open stood;
But therein sat an amiable dame,
That seemed to be of very sober mood,
And in her semblant showed great womanhood:
Strange was her tire; for on her head a crown
She wore much like unto a Danish hood,
Powdered with pearl and stone, and all her gown
Enwoven was with gold, that raught full low adown.

29.9 **all were they** even if they were　30.6 **king** Solomon　31.5
**semblant** appearance　.6 **tire** attire　.8 **powdered** sprinkled
.9 **raught** reached

32]  On either side of her, two young men stood,
Both strongly armed, as fearing one another;
Yet were they brethren both, of half the blood,
Begotten by two fathers of one mother,
Though of contrary natures each to other;
The one of them hight Love, the other Hate:
Hate was the elder, Love the younger brother;
Yet was the younger stronger in his state
Than th'elder, and him mastered still in all debate.

33]  Nath'less that dame so well them tempered both
That she them forcéd hand to join in hand,
Albe that Hatred was thereto full loath,
And turned his face away, as he did stand,
Unwilling to behold that lovely band.
Yet she was of such grace and virtuous might,
That her commandment he could not withstand,
But bit his lip for felonous despite,
And gnashed his iron tusks at that displeasing sight.

34]  Concord she clepéd was in common rede,
Mother of blesséd Peace and Friendship true:
They both her twins, both born of heavenly seed;
And she herself likewise divinely grew,
The which right well her works divine did shew:
For strength and wealth and happiness she lends,
And strife and war and anger does subdue;
Of little, much; of foes, she maketh friends;
And to afflicted minds sweet rest and quiet sends.

35]  By her the heaven is in his course contained,
And all the world in state unmovéd stands,
As their Almighty Maker first ordained,
And bound them with inviolable bands;
Else would the waters overflow the lands
And fire devour the air, and hell them quite;
But that she holds them with her blesséd hands.

---

**33.5 lovely band**  loving bond   **34.1 common rede**  usual speech
**35.6 hell them quite**  hell punish them, i.e., everything would
return to chaos

She is the nurse of pleasure and delight,
And unto Venus' grace the gate doth open right.

36] By her I entering half dismayéd was,
But she in gentle wise me entertained,
And 'twixt herself and Love did let me pass;
But Hatred would my entrance have restrained,
And with his club me threatened to have brained,
Had not the lady with her powerful speech
Him from his wicked will uneath refrained;
And th'other eke his malice did empeach
Till I was throughly past the peril of his reach.

37] Into the inmost temple thus I came,
Which fuming all with frankincense I found,
And odors rising from the altar's flame.
Upon an hundred marble pillars round
The roof up high was rearéd from the ground,
All decked with crowns and chains and garlands gay,
And thousand precious gifts worth many a pound,
The which sad lovers for their vows did pay;
And all the ground was strewed with flowers, as fresh as
    May.

38] An hundred altars round about were set,
All flaming with their sacrifices' fire,
That with the steam thereof the temple sweat,
Which, rolled in clouds, to heaven did aspire,
And in them bore true lovers' vows entire:
And eke an hundred brazen cauldrons bright,
To bathe in joy and amorous delight,
Every of which was to a damsel hight:
For all the priests were damsels, in soft linen dight.

39] Right in the midst the goddess self did stand
Upon an altar of some costly mass,
Whose substance was uneath to understand:
For neither precious stone, nor dureful brass,

36.7 **uneath** with difficulty   .8 **empeach** impede   .9 **throughly**
thoroughly   37.8 **sad** true   38.8 **hight** assigned   39.4 **dureful**
enduring

Nor shining gold, nor moldering clay it was;
But much more rare and precious to esteem,
Pure in aspect, and like to crystal glass—
Yet glass was not, if one did rightly deem,
But being fair and brickle, likest glass did seem.

40] But it in shape and beauty did excel
All other idols which the heathen adore;
Far passing that, which by surpassing skill
Phidias did make in Paphos Isle of yore,
With which that wretched Greek, that life forlore,
Did fall in love: yet this much fairer shined,
But covered with a slender veil afore;
And both her feet and legs together twined
Were with a snake, whose head and tail were fast combined.

41] The cause why she was covered with a veil
Was hard to know, for that her priests the same
From people's knowledge labored to conceal.
But sooth it was not sure for womanish shame,
Nor any blemish, which the work mote blame;
But for, they say, she hath both kinds in one,
Both male and female, both under one name:
She sire and mother is herself alone,
Begets and eke conceives, nor needeth other none.

42] And all about her neck and shoulders flew
A flock of little loves, and sports and joys,
With nimble wings of gold and purple hue,
Whose shapes seemed not like to terrestial boys,
But like to angels playing heavenly toys,
The whilst their eldest brother was away—
Cupid, their eldest brother; he enjoys
The wide kingdom of love with lordly sway,
And to his law compels all creatures to obey.

43] And all about her altar scattered lay
Great sorts of lovers piteously complaining:

40.5–6 **Greek . . . love** as was told of the Aphrodite of Cnidos
by Praxiteles

Some of their loss, some of their love's delay,
Some of their pride, some paragons' disdaining,
Some fearing fraud, some fraudulently feigning,
As every one had cause of good or ill.
Amongst the rest, some one, through love's constraining
Tormented sore, could not contain it still,
But thus brake forth, that all the temple it did fill:

44] Great Venus, queen of beauty and of grace,
The joy of gods and men, that under sky
Dost fairest shine and most adorn thy place,
That with thy smiling look dost pacify
The raging seas, and mak'st the storms to fly:
Thee goddess, thee the winds, the clouds do fear,
And when thou spreadst thy mantle forth on high,
The waters play and pleasant lands appear,
And heavens laugh, and all the world shows joyous cheer.

45] Then doth the daedal earth throw forth to thee
Out of her fruitful lap abundant flowers,
And then all living wights, soon as they see
The spring break forth out of his lusty bowers,
They all do learn to play the paramours:
First do the merry birds, thy pretty pages,
Privily prickéd with thy lustful powers,
Chirp loud to thee out of their leavy cages,
And thee their mother call to cool their kindly rages;

46] Then do the savage beasts begin to play
Their pleasant frisks, and loathe their wonted food;
The lions roar, the tigers loudly bray,
The raging bulls rebellow through the wood,
And breaking forth, dare tempt the deepest flood,
To come where thou dost draw them with desire;
So all things else that nourish vital blood,
Soon as with fury thou dost them inspire,
In generation seek to quench their inward fire.

43.4 **paragons'** mates'   44.3–5 **Dost . . . fly** as the planet
Venus traditionally does

47]  So all the world by thee at first was made,
And daily yet thou dost the same repair;
Ne aught on earth that merry is and glad,
Ne aught on earth that lovely is and fair,
But thou the same for pleasure didst prepare.
Thou art the root of all that joyous is:
Great god of men and women, queen of th'air,
Mother of laughter and wellspring of bliss:
O grant that of my love at last I may not miss!

48]  So did he say: but I with murmur soft,
That none might hear the sorrow of my heart,
Yet inly groaning deep and sighing oft,
Besought her to grant ease unto my smart,
And to my wound her gracious help impart.
Whilst thus I spake, behold! with happy eye
I spied where at the idol's feet apart
A bevy of fair damsels close did lie,
Waiting whenas the anthem should be sung on high.

49]  The first of them did seem of riper years
And graver countenance than all the rest:
Yet all the rest were eke her equal peers;
Yet unto her obeyéd all the best.
Her name was Womanhood, that she expressed
By her sad semblant and demeanor wise;
For steadfast still her eyes did fixéd rest,
Nor roved at random after gazer's guise,
Whose luring baits oft times do heedless hearts entice.

50]  And next to her sat goodly Shamefastness,
Ne ever durst her eyes from ground uprear,
Ne ever once did look up from her dais,
As if some blame of evil she did fear,
That in her cheeks made roses oft appear;
And her against sweet Cheerfulness was placed,
Whose eyes like twinkling stars in evening clear
Were decked with smiles, that all sad humors chased,
And darted forth delights, the which her goodly graced.

45.1 **daedal** fertile   49.8 **guise** fashion   50.6 **against** opposite

51] And next to her sat sober Modesty,
Holding her hand upon her gentle heart;
And her against sat comely Courtesy,
That unto every person knew her part;
And her before was seated overthwart
Soft Silence, and submiss Obedience,
Both linked together never to dispart—
Both gifts of God not gotten but from thence,
Both garlands of his saints against their foes' offence.

52] Thus sat they all around in seemly rate;
And in the midst of them a goodly maid,
Even in the lap of Womanhood there sate,
The which was all in lily white arrayed,
With silver streams amongst the linen strayed:
Like to the morn, when first her shining face
Hath to the gloomy world itself bewrayed;
That same was fairest Amoret in place,
Shining with beauty's light, and heavenly virtue's grace.

53] Whom soon as I beheld, my heart gan throb,
And wade in doubt, what best were to be done:
For sacrilege me seemed the church to rob,
And folly seemed to leave the thing undone,
Which with so strong attempt I had begun.
Tho shaking off all doubt and shamefast fear,
Which lady's love I heard had never won
'Mongst men of worth, I to her steppéd near,
And by the lily hand her labored up to rear.

54] Thereat that foremost matron me did blame
And sharp rebuke, for being over bold,
Saying it was to knight unseemly shame
Upon a recluse virgin to lay hold,
That unto Venus' services was sold.
To whom I thus: Nay, but it fitteth best,
For Cupid's man with Venus' maid to hold,
For ill your goddess' services are dressed
By virgins, and her sacrifices let to rest.

51.4 **her part** i.e., how to behave   .5 **overthwart** opposite
52.1 **rate** manner

55] With that my shield I forth to her did show,
Which all that while I closely had concealed;
On which when Cupid with his killing bow
And cruel shafts emblazoned she beheld,
At sight thereof she was with terror quelled,
And said no more; but I which all that while
The pledge of faith, her hand, engagéd held,
Like wary hind within the weedy soil,
For no entreaty would forego so glorious spoil.

56] And evermore upon the goddess' face
Mine eye was fixed, for fear of her offence;
Whom when I saw with amiable grace
To laugh at me, and favor my pretence,
I was emboldened with more confidence,
And naught for niceness nor for envy sparing,
In presence of them all forth led her thence:
All looking on, and like astonished staring;
Yet to lay hand on her, not one of all them daring.

57] She often prayed, and often me besought,
Sometime with tender tears to let her go,
Sometimes with witching smiles: but yet for naught
That ever she to me could say or do,
Could she her wishéd freedom from me woo;
But forth I led her through the temple gate,
By which I hardly passed with much ado:
But that same lady which me friended late
In entrance, did me also friend in my retreat.

58] No less did Danger threaten me with dread,
Whenas he saw me, maugre all his power,
That glorious spoil of beauty with me lead,
Than Cerberus, when Orpheus did recower
His leman from the Stygian prince's bower.

55.8 **Like . . . soil** like a deer hiding in weedy growth   56.4
**pretence** pretension   .6 **niceness** scrupulousness   .8 **like**
equally   57.7 **hardly** with difficulty   58.4 **recower** recover   .5
**leman** beloved

But evermore my shield did me defend
Against the storm of every dreadful stour:
Thus safely with my love I thence did wend.
So ended he his tale, where I this canto end.

.7 **stour**  danger

# Book VI

## Canto ix

Sir Calidore *is the hero of the book of courtesy: the civil behavior which makes relationships between men gracious. Engaged in his quest for the* Blatant Beast (*scandal, the enemy of courteous relationships*), *Calidore finds himself in a rural and pastoral situation, far from courts and civil life. Yet here he finds the Graces.* [Eds.]

5] There on a day as he pursued the chase,
He chanced to spy a sort of shepherd grooms,
Playing on pipes, and caroling apace,
The whiles their beasts there in the budded brooms
Beside them fed, and nipped the tender blooms:
For other worldly wealth they caréd naught.
To whom Sir Calidore yet sweating comes,
And them to tell him courteously besought,
If such a beast they saw, which he had thither brought.

6] They answered him that no such beast they saw,
Nor any wicked fiend that mote offend
Their happy flocks, nor danger to them draw:
But if that such there were (as none they kenned)
They prayed high God him far from them to send.
Then one of them him seeing so to sweat,
After his rustic wise, that well he weened,
Offered him drink, to quench his thirsty heat,
And if he hungry were, him offered eke to eat.

7] The knight was nothing nice, where was no need,
And took their gentle offer: so adown
They prayed him sit, and gave him for to feed
Such homely what as serves the simple clown,

5.3 **caroling** singing  7.1 **nice** fussy, finicking  .4 **clown** peasant

That doth despise the dainties of the town.
Tho having fed his fill, he there beside
Saw a fair damsel, which did wear a crown
Of sundry flowers, with silken ribbons tied,
Yclad in home-made green that her own hands had dyed.

8] Upon a little hillock she was placed
Higher than all the rest, and roundabout
Environed with a garland, goodly graced,
Of lovely lasses, and them all without
The lusty shepherd swains sat in a rout,
The which did pipe and sing her praises due,
And oft rejoice, and oft for wonder shout,
As if some miracle of heavenly hue
Were down to them descended in that earthly view.

9] And soothly sure she was full fair of face,
And perfectly well shaped in every limb,
Which she did more augment with modest grace,
And comely carriage of her count'nance trim,
That all the rest like lesser lamps did dim:
Who, her admiring as some heavenly wight,
Did for their sovereign goddess her esteem,
And caroling her name both day and night,
The fairest Pastorella her by name did hight.

10] Nor was there herd, nor was there shepherd's swain
But did her honor, and eke many a one
Burned in her love, and with sweet pleasing pain
Full many a night for her did sigh and groan:
But most of all the shepherd Corydon
For her did languish, and his dear life spend;
Yet neither she for him, nor other none,
Did care a whit, ne any liking lend:
Though mean her lot, yet higher did her mind ascend.

11] Her whiles Sir Calidore there viewéd well,
And marked her rare demeanor, which him seemed
So far the mean of shepherd's to excel

.6 **Tho** then  8.5 **rout** crowd  9.9 **hight** call  10.9 **mean**
lowly  11.3 **mean** average

As that he in his mind her worthy deemed
To be a prince's paragon esteemed,
He was unwares surprised in subtle bands
Of the blind boy, nor thence could be redeemed
By any skill out of his cruel hands:
Caught like the bird, which gazing still on others stands.

12]　So stood he still long gazing thereupon,
Ne any will had thence to move away,
Although his quest were far afore him gone;
But after he had fed, yet did he stay,
And sat there still, until the flying day
Was far forth spent, discoursing diversly
Of sundry things, as fell, to work delay;
And evermore his speech he did apply
To th'herds, but meant them to the damsel's fantasy.

13]　By this, the moisty night approaching fast,
Her dewy humor gan on th'earth to shed,
That warned the shepherds to their homes to haste
Their tender flocks, now being fully fed,
For fear of wetting them before their bed;
Then came to them a good old aged sire,
Whose silver locks bedecked his beard and head,
With shepherd's hook in hand, and fit attire,
That willed the damsel rise; the day did now expire.

14]　He was, to wit, by common voice esteemed
The father of the fairest Pastorell,
And of herself in very deed so deemed:
Yet was not so; but as old stories tell
Found her by fortune, which to him befell,
In th'open fields an infant left alone,
And taking up brought home, and nurséd well
As his own child—for other he had none—
That she in track of time accounted was his own.

.5 **paragon** mate  .7 **boy** Cupid  .9 **bird** larks were sometimes
trapped when their attention had been distracted by a hawk
or a mirror  12.7 **fell** chanced  .9 **fantasy** understanding  14.1
**common voice** general opinion

15]    She at his bidding meekly did arise,
     And straight unto her little flock did fare;
     Then all the rest about her rose likewise,
     And each his sundry sheep with several care
     Gathered together, and them homeward bare:
     Whilst every one with helping hands did strive
     Amongst themselves, and did their labors share,
     To help fair Pastorella home to drive
     Her fleecy flock; but Corydon most help did give.

16]    But Melibee (so hight that good old man)
     Now seeing Calidore left all alone
     And night arrivéd hard at hand, began
     Him to invite unto his simple home;
     Which, though it were a cottage clad with loam,
     And all things therein mean, yet better so
     To lodge than in the savage fields to roam.
     The knight full gladly soon agreed thereto,
     Being his heart's own wish, and home with him did go.

17]    There he was welcomed of that honest sire,
     And of his agéd beldame homely well;
     Who him besought himself to disattire,
     And rest himself, till supper time befell.
     By which home came the fairest Pastorell,
     After her flock she in their fold had tied;
     And supper ready dight, they to it fell
     With small ado, and nature satisfied,
     The which doth little crave, contented to abide.

18]    Tho when they had their hunger slakéd well,
     And the fair maid the table ta'en away,
     The gentle knight, as he that did excel
     In courtesy, and well could do and say,
     For so great kindness as he found that day
     Gan greatly thank his host and his good wife;
     And drawing thence his speech another way,

---

17.2 **beldame** aged lady    .9 **contented to abide** in order to be contented

Gan highly to commend the happy life
Which shepherds lead, without debate or bitter strife.

19]   How much (said he) more happy is the state
In which ye, father, here do dwell at ease,
Leading a life so free and fortunate,
From all the tempests of these worldly seas,
Which toss the rest in dangerous disease,
Where wars, and wrecks, and wicked enmity
Do them afflict, which no man can appease;
That certes I your happiness envy,
And wish my lot were placed in such felicity.

20]   Surely, my son (then answered he again),
If happy, then it is in this intent:
That having small, yet do I not complain
Of want, ne wish for more it to augment,
But do myself with that I have content;
So taught of nature, which doth little need
Of foreign helps to life's due nourishment:
The fields my food, my flock my raiment breed;
No better do I wear, no better do I feed.

21]   Therefore I do not anyone envy,
Nor am envied of any one therefore;
They that have much, fear much to lose thereby,
And store of cares doth follow riches' store.
The little that I have grows daily more
Without my care, but only to attend it;
My lambs do every year increase their score,
And my flock's father daily doth amend it.
What have I, but to praise th'Almighty, that doth send it?

22]   To them that list, the world's gay shows I leave,
And to great ones such follies do forgive,
Which oft through pride do their own peril weave,
And through ambition down themselves do drive
To sad decay, that might contented live.
Me no such cares nor cumbrous thoughts offend,
Ne once my mind's unmovéd quiet grieve,

20.2 **intent** sense   22.1 **list** wish   .2 **forgive** give over

But all the night in silver sleep I spend,
And all the day, to what I list, I do attend.

23] Sometimes I hunt the fox, the vowéd foe
Unto my lambs, and him dislodge away;
Sometime the fawn I practise from the doe,
Or from the goat her kid, how to convey;
Another while I baits and nets display,
The birds to catch, or fishes to beguile:
And when I weary am, I down do lay
My limbs in every shade, to rest from toil,
And drink of every brook, when thirst my throat doth boil.

24] The time was once, in my first prime of years,
When pride of youth forth prickéd my desire,
That I disdained amongst mine equal peers
To follow sheep, and shepherd's base attire;
For further fortune then I would inquire.
And leaving home, to royal court I sought,
Where I did sell myself for yearly hire,
And in the prince's garden daily wrought:
There I beheld such vainness as I never thought.

25] With sight whereof soon cloyed, and long deluded
With idle hopes, which them do entertain,
After I had ten years my self excluded
From native home, and spent my youth in vain,
I gan my follies to myself to plain,
And this sweet peace, whose lack did then appear.
Tho back returning to my sheep again,
I from thenceforth have learned to love more dear
This lowly quiet life which I inherit here.

26] Whilst thus he talked, the knight with greedy ear
Hung still upon his melting mouth attent;
Whose senseful words empierced his heart so near
That he was rapt with double ravishment:
Both of his speech that wrought him great content,

25.2 **them do entertain** occupy them   .5 **plain** mourn   26.2
**attent** attentive

And also of the object of his view,
On which his hungry eye was always bent;
That 'twixt his pleasing tongue, and her fair hue,
He lost himself, and like one half entrancéd grew.

27]  Yet to occasion means to work his mind,
And to insinuate his heart's desire,
He thus replied: Now surely sire, I find,
That all this world's gay shows, which we admire,
Be but vain shadows to this safe retire
Of life, which here in lowliness ye lead,
Fearless of foes, or fortune's wreakful ire,
Which tosseth states, and under foot doth tread
The mighty ones, afraid of every chance's dread.

28]  That even I which daily do behold
The glory of the great, 'mongst which I won,
And now haved proved what happiness ye hold
In this small plot of your dominión
Now loathe great lordship and ambitión,
And wish the heavens so much had gracéd me.
As grant me live in like conditión;
Or that my fortunes might transposéd be
From pitch of higher place, unto this low degree.

29]  In vain (said then old Melibee) do men
The heavens of their fortune's fault accuse,
Sith they know best what is the best for them:
For they to each such fortune do diffuse
As they do know each can most aptly use.
For not that which men covet most is best,
Nor that thing worst, which men do most refuse;
But fittest is, that all contented rest
With that they hold: each hath his fortune in his breast.

30]  It is the mind that maketh good or ill,
That maketh wretch or happy, rich or poor:
For some that hath abundance at his will,
Hath not enough, but wants in greatest store;
And other, that hath little, asks no more,

27.1 **occasion** produce   .7 **wreakful** avenging   28.2 **won**
dwell   .3 **proved** experienced   29.3 **they** heavens

But in that little is both rich and wise.
For wisdom is most riches; fools therefore
They are, which fortunes do by vows devise,
Since each unto himself his life may fortunize.

31] Since then in each man's self (said Calidore)
It is, to fashion his own life's estate,
Give leave awhile, good father, in this shore
To rest my bark, which hath been beaten late
With storms of fortune and tempestuous fate,
In seas of troubles and of toilsome pain,
That whether quite from them for to retreat
I shall resolve, or back to turn again,
I may here with yourself some small repose obtain.

32] Not that the burden of so bold a guest
Shall chargeful be, or change to you at all;
For your mean food shall be my daily feast,
And this your cabin both my bower and hall;
Besides for recompense hereof, I shall
You well reward, and golden guerdon give,
That may perhaps you better much withal,
And in this quiet make you safer live.
—So forth he drew much gold, and tóward him it drive.

33] But the good man, naught tempted with the offer
Of his rich mold, did thrust it far away,
And thus bespake: Sir knight, your bounteous proffer
Be far from me, to whom ye ill display
That mucky mass, the cause of men's decay,
That mote impair my peace with dangers dread.
But if ye algates covet to assay
This simple sort of life that shepherds lead,
Be it your own: our rudeness to yourself aread.

34] So there that night Sir Calidore did dwell,
And long while after, whilst him list remain,

30.8 **by vows devise** try to get by vow or prayer   31.4 **bark**
ship   32.4 **bower and hall** rooms for day and night   .9 **drive**
pushed   33.2 **mold** dirt, i.e., gold   .7 **algates** at all   .9 **aread**
take

Daily beholding the fair Pastorell,
And feeding on the bait of his own bane.
During which time he did her entertain
With all kind courtesies he could invent;
And every day, her company to gain,
When to the field she went, he with her went;
So for to quench his fire, he did it more augment.

35]    But she, that never had acquainted been
With such quaint usage, fit for queens and kings,
Nor ever had such knightly service seen,
But, being bred under base shepherd's wings,
Had ever learned to love the lowly things,
Did little whit regard his courteous guise,
But caréd more for Colin's carolings
Than all that he could do, or e'er devise:
His lays, his loves, his looks—she did them all despise.

36]    Which Calidore perceiving, thought it best
To change the manner of his lofty look;
And doffing his bright arms, himself addressed
In shepherd's weed, and in his hand he took,
Instead of steelhead spear, a shepherd's hook,
That who had seen him then would have bethought
On Phrygian Paris by Plexippus brook,
When he the love of fair Oenone sought,
What time the golden apple was unto him brought.

37]    So being clad, unto the fields he went
With the fair Pastorella every day,
And kept her sheep with diligent attent,
Watching to drive the ravenous wolf away,
The whilst at pleasure she mote sport and play;
And every evening helping them to fold;
And otherwise, for need, he did assay
In his strong hand their rugged teats to hold,
And out of them to press the milk: love so much could.

38]    Which seeing, Corydon, who her likewise
Long time had loved, and hoped her love to gain,

35.6 **guise**  manner

He much was troubled at that stranger's guise,
And many jealous thoughts conceived in vain,
That this of all his labor and long pain
Should reap the harvest, ere it ripened were;
That made him scowl, and pout, and oft complain
Of Pastorell to all the shepherds there,
That she did love a stranger swain than him more dear.

39] And ever when he came in company
Where Calidore was present, he would lower,
And bite his lip, and even for jealousy
Was ready oft his own heart to devour,
Impatiént of any paramour:
Who on the other side did seem so far
From malicing, or grudging his good hour,
That all he could, he gracéd him with her,
Nor ever showéd sign of rancor or of ire.

40] And oft, when Corydon unto her brought
Or little sparrows, stolen from their nest,
Or wanton squirrels, in the woods far sought,
Or other dainty thing for her addressed,
He would commend his gift, and make the best.
Yet she no whit his presents did regard,
Nor him could find to fancy in her breast:
This new-come shepherd had his market marred.
Old love is little worth when new is more preferred.

41] One day whenas the shepherd swains together
Were met, to make their sports and merry glee,
As they are wont in fair sunshiny weather,
The whiles their flocks in shadows shrouded be,
They fell to dance: then did they all agree,
That Colin Clout should pipe as one most fit;
And Calidore should lead the ring, as he
That most in Pastorella's grace did sit.
Thereat frowned Corydon, and his lip closely bit.

39.5 **paramour** rival lover  40.2 **Or** either  .8 **his** Corydon's

42]   But Calidore, of courteous inclination,
    Took Corydon, and set him in his place,
    That he should lead the dance, as was his fashion,
    For Corydon could dance and trimly trace;
    And whenas Pastorella, him to grace,
    Her flowery garland took from her own head,
    And placed on his, he did it soon displace,
    And did it put on Corydon's instead;
    Then Corydon wox frolic, that erst seeméd dead.

43]   Another time, whenas they did dispose
    To practice games, and masteries to try,
    They for their judge did Pastorella choose;
    A garland was the meed of victory.
    There Corydon, forth stepping openly,
    Did challenge Calidore to wrestling game:
    For he through long and perfect industry,
    Therein well practiced was, and in the same
    Thought sure t'avenge his grudge, and work his foe great
        shame.

44]   But Calidore he greatly did mistake,
    For he was strong and mightily stiff pight,
    That with one fall his neck he almost brake,
    And had he not upon him fallen light,
    His dearest joint he sure had broken quite.
    Then was the oaken crown by Pastorell
    Given to Calidore, as his due right;
    But he, that did in courtesy excel,
    Gave it to Corydon, and said he won it well.

45]   Thus did the gentle knight himself abear
    Amongst that rustic rout in all his deeds,
    That even they, the which his rivals were,
    Could not malign him, but commend him needs;
    For courtesy amongst the rudest breeds
    Good will and favor. So it surely wrought

42.4 **trace** step   43.2 **masteries to try** hold contests   44.2
**stiff pight** firmly put together   45.4 **needs** necessarily

With this fair maid, and in her mind the seeds
Of perfect love did sow, that last forth brought
The fruit of joy and bliss, though long time dearly bought.

## Canto x

1]  Who now does follow the foul Blatant Beast,
    Whilst Calidore does follow that fair maid,
    Unmindful of his vow and high behest,
    Which by the Faery Queen was on him laid,
    That he should never leave, nor be delayed
    From chasing him, till he had it achieved?
    But now entrapped of love, which him betrayed,
    He mindeth more how he may be relieved
    With  grace  from  her  whose  love  his  heart  hath  sore
         engrieved,

2]  That from henceforth he means no more to sue
    His former quest, so full of toil and pain;
    Another quest, another game in view
    He hath, the guerdon of his love to gain:
    With whom he minds forever to remain,
    And set his rest among the rustic sort,
    Rather than hunt still after shadows vain
    Of courtly favor, fed with light report
    Of every blast, and sailing always on the port.

3]  Ne certes mote he greatly blaméd be,
    From so high step to stoop unto so low;
    For who had tasted once (as oft did he)
    The happy peace, which there doth overflow,
    And proved the perfect pleasures which do grow
    Amongst poor hinds, in hills, in woods, in dales,
    Would never more delight in painted show
    Of such false bliss, as there is set for stales,
    T'entrap unwary fools in their eternal bales.

.8 **last**  at last   2.1 **sue**  follow   .6 **set his rest**  base himself   .9
**on the port**  possibly "on the port tack," when a ship must yield
right-of-way to others   3.8 **stales**  snares   .9 **bales**  misfortunes

4]  For what hath all that goodly glorious gaze
    Like to one sight which Calidore did view?
    That glance whereof their dimméd eyes would daze,
    That nevermore they should endure the show
    Of that sunshine that makes them look askew.
    Ne aught in all that world of beauties rare
    (Save only Gloriana's heavenly hue,
    To which what can compare?) can it compare;
    The which as cometh now, by course I will declare.

5]  One day as he did range the fields abroad,
    Whilst his fair Pastorella was elsewhere,
    He chanced to come, far from all people's trod,
    Unto a place whose pleasance did appear
    To pass all others on the earth which were:
    For all that ever was by nature's skill
    Devised to work delight, was gathered there,
    And there by her were pouréd forth at fill:
    As if this to adorn, she all the rest did pill.

6]  It was a hill placed in an open plain,
    That roundabout was bordered with a wood
    Of matchless height, that seemed th'earth to disdain,
    In which all trees of honor stately stood,
    And did all winter as in summer bud,
    Spreading pavilions for the birds to bower,
    Which in their lower branches sung aloud;
    And in their tops the soaring hawk did tower,
    Sitting like king of fowls in majesty and power.

7]  And at the foot thereof, a gentle flood
    His silver waves did softly tumble down,
    Unmarred with ragged moss or filthy mud;
    Ne mote wild beasts, ne mote the ruder clown
    Thereto approach, ne filth mote therein drown:
    But nymphs and faeries by the banks did sit,
    In the wood's shade, which did the waters crown,

4.7 **Gloriana**  the Faerie Queene; also Elizabeth I   .8 **it compare**
compare with it   5.3 **trod**  footsteps   .9 **pill**  pillage, plunder

Keeping all noisome things away from it,
And to the water's fall tuning their accents fit.

8] And on the top thereof a spacious plain
Did spread itself, to serve to all delight,
Either to dance, when they to dance would fain,
Or else to course about their bases light;
Ne aught there wanted which for pleasure might
Desired be, or thence to banish bale,
So pleasantly the hill with equal height,
Did seem to overlook the lowly vale;
Therefore it rightly clepéd was Mount Acidale.

9] They say that Venus, when she did dispose
Herself to pleasance, uséd to resort
Unto this place, and therein to repose
And rest herself, as in a gladsome port,
Or with the Graces there to play and sport;
That even her own Cytheron, though in it
She uséd most to keep her royal court,
And in her sovereign majesty to sit,
She in regard hereof refused and thought unfit.

10] Unto this place whenas the Elfin knight
Approached, him seeméd that the merry sound
Of a shrill pipe he playing heard on height,
And many feet fast thumping th'hollow ground,
That through the woods their echo did rebound.
He nigher drew, to weet what mote it be;
There he a troop of ladies dancing found
Full merrily, and making gladful glee,
And in the midst a shepherd piping he did see.

11] He durst not enter into th'open green,
For dread of them unwares to be descried,
For breaking of their dance, if he were seen;

8.4 **course . . . bases** play the game of prisoner's base  .9
**clepéd** called  **Acidale** a place sacred to Venus and the graces
9.9 **in regard hereof** in comparison with this   10.1 **Elfin knight**
Calidore (a knight of the Faerie Queene)  .2 **him seeméd** it
seemed to him  .6 **weet** learn  11.3 **for . . . dance** lest their
dance break up

But in the covert of the wood did bide,
Beholding all, yet of them unespied.
There he did see that pleaséd much his sight,
That even he himself his eyes envied:
An hundred naked maidens, lily white,
All rangéd in a ring, and dancing in delight.

12] All they without were rangéd in a ring,
And danced round; but in the midst of them
Three other ladies did both dance and sing,
The whilst the rest them roundabout did hem,
And like a garland did in compass stem:
And in the midst of those same three, was placed
Another damsel, as a precious gem,
Amidst a ring most richly well enchased,
That with her goodly presence all the rest much graced.

13] Look how the crown which Ariadne wore
Upon her ivory forehead, that same day
That Theseus her unto his bridal bore—
When the bold centaurs made that bloody fray,
With the fierce lapiths, which did them dismay—
Being now placéd in the firmament,
Through the bright heaven doth her beams display,
And is unto the stars an ornament,
Which round about her move in order excellent.

14] Such was the beauty of this goodly band,
Whose sundry parts were here too long to tell:
But she that in the midst of them did stand
Seemed all the rest in beauty to excel,
Crowned with a rosy garland, that right well
Did her beseem. And ever, as the crew
About her danced, sweet flowers, that far did smell,
And fragrant odors they upon her threw;
But most of all those three did her with gifts endue.

12.5 **in compass stem** confine in a circle  .8 **enchased** set (like
a gem)  13.1 **Ariadne** the marriage seems to be confused with
another, and the constellation Corona Borealis seems to be put in
the place of the North Star, around which the other stars circle

15] Those were the Graces, daughters of delight,
Handmaids of Venus, which are wont to haunt
Upon this hill, and dance there day and night:
Those three to men all gifts of grace do grant,
And all that Venus in herself doth vaunt
Is borrowed of them. But that fair one
That in the midst was placéd paramount
Was she to whom that shepherd piped alone,
That made him pipe so merrily as never none.

16] She was, to wit, that jolly shepherd's lass,
Which pipéd there unto that merry rout;
That jolly shepherd, which there pipéd, was
Poor Colin Clout (who knows not Colin Clout?):
He piped apace, whilst they him danced about.
Pipe, jolly shepherd, pipe thou now apace
Unto thy love, that made thee low to lout:
Thy love is present there with thee in place,
Thy love is there advanced to be another Grace.

17] Much wondered Calidore at this strange sight,
Whose like before his eye had never seen,
And standing long astonishéd in spright,
And rapt with pleasance, wist not what to ween:
Whether it were the train of beauty's queen,
Or nymphs, or faeries, or enchanted show,
With which his eyes mote have deluded been.
Therefore, resolving what it was to know,
Out of the wood he rose, and toward them did go.

18] But soon as he appearéd to their view,
They vanished all away out of his sight,
And clean were gone, which way he never knew;
All save the shepherd, who for fell despite
Of that displeasure, broke his bagpipe quite,
And made great moan for that unhappy turn.
But Calidore, though no less sorry wight,

16.2 **Which** the shepherd  .4 **Colin Clout** a pseudonym for
Spenser  .7 **lout** bow  17.3 **spright** spirit  .4 **ween** think

For that mishap, yet seeing him to mourn,
Drew near, that he the truth of all by him mote learn.

19] And first him greeting, thus, unto him spake:
Hail, jolly shepherd, which thy joyous days
Here leadest in this goodly merry-make,
Frequented of these gentle nymphs always,
Which to thee flock to hear thy lovely lays;
Tell me, what mote these dainty damsels be,
Which here with thee do make their pleasant plays?
Right happy thou, that mayst them freely see:
But why when I them saw, fled they away from me?

20] Not I so happy, answered then that swain,
As thou unhappy which them thence did chase,
Whom by no means thou canst recall again,
For being gone, none can them bring in place,
But whom they of themselves list so to grace.
Right sorry I (said then Sir Calidore)
That my ill fortune did them hence displace.
But since things passéd none may now restore,
Tell me, what were they all, whose lack thee grieves so
sore?

21] Tho gan that shepherd thus for to dilate:
That all these ladies, which thou sawest late,
Then wote thou, shepherd, whatsoever thou be,
Are Venus' damsels, all within her fee,
But differing in honor and degree;
They all are Graces, which on her depend,
Besides a thousand more, which ready be
Her to adorn, when so she forth doth wend:
But those three in the midst do chief on her attend.

22] They are the daughters of sky-ruling Jove,
By him begot of fair Eurynome,
The Ocean's daughter, in this pleasant grove,
As he this way coming from feastful glee,
Of Thetis' wedding with Aeacidee,
In summer's shade himself here rested weary.

21.2 **wote** know   .4 **fee** service   22.5 **Aeacidee** Peleus

The first of them hight mild Euphrosyne,
Next fair Aglaia, last Thalia merry:
Sweet goddesses all three, which me in mirth do cherry.

23]  These three on men all gracious gifts bestow
Which deck the body or adorn the mind,
To make them lovely or well-favored show,
As comely carriage, entertainment kind,
Sweet semblant, friendly offices that bind,
And all the complements of courtesy:
They teach us how to each degree and kind
We should ourselves demean—to low, to high,
To friends, to foes—which skill men call civility.

24]  Therefore they always smoothly seem to smile,
That we likewise should mild and gentle be,
And also naked are, that without guile
Or false dissemblance all them plain may see.
Simple and true, from covert malice free;
And eke themselves so in their dance they bore,
That two of them still towards seemed to be,
But one still froward showed herself afore:
That good should from us go, then come in greater store.

25]  Such were those goddesses, which ye did see;
But that fourth maid, which there amidst them traced,
Who can aread what creature mote she be,
Whether a creature, or a goddess graced
With heavenly gifts from heaven first enraced?
But what so sure she was, she worthy was
To be the fourth with those three other, placed:
Yet was she certes but a country lass—
Yet she all other country lasses far did pass.

26]  So far as doth the daughter of the day
All other lesser lights in light excel,
So far doth she in beautiful array

.9 **cherry** cheer   23.5 **semblant** demeanor   .8 **demean** behave
24.7–8 **two . . . afore** two face the onlooker, while the third, in
front, has her back turned   25.3 **aread** tell   .5 **enraced** im-
planted   26.1 **daughter . . . day** Venus as Morning Star

Above all other lasses bear the bell:
Ne less in virtue that beseems her well,
Doth she exceed the rest of all her race;
For which the Graces that here wont to dwell,
Have for more honor brought her to this place,
And gracéd her so much to be another Grace.

27] Another Grace she well deserves to be,
In whom so many graces gathered are,
Excelling much the mean of her degree:
Divine resemblance, beauty sovereign rare,
Firm chastity, that spite ne blemish dare:
All which she with such courtesy doth grace,
That all her peers cannot with her compare,
But quite are dimméd when she is in place.
She made me often pipe and now to pipe apace.

28] Sun of the world, great glory of the sky,
That all the earth dost lighten with thy rays,
Great Gloriana, greatest majesty,
Pardon thy shepherd, 'mongst so many lays
As he hath sung of thee in all his days,
To make one minim of thy poor handmaid,
And underneath thy feet to place her praise,
That when thy glory shall be far displayed
To future age, of her this mention may be made.

29] When thus that shepherd ended had his speech,
Said Calidore: Now sure it irketh me,
That to thy bliss I made this luckless breach,
As now the author of thy bale to be,
Thus to bereave thy love's dear sight from thee:
But, gentle shepherd, pardon thou my shame,
Who rashly sought that which I mote not see.
—Thus did the courteous knight excuse his blame,
And to recomfort him, all comely means did frame.

.4 **bear the bell** take first place   27.3 **mean** average   28.6
**minim** a short musical note, a small amount

# bibliography

## editions

*The Works of Edmund Spenser: A Variorum Edition*, E. Greenlaw and others, eds., 9 vols. (Baltimore, 1932–49) [voluminous commentary; the standard edition].

*The Complete Poetical Works of Edmund Spenser*, R. E. Neil Dodge, ed. (Boston, 1908) [Houghton Mifflin "Student's Cambridge Edition"].

*The Poetical Works of Edmund Spenser*, J. C. Smith and E. de Selincourt, eds. (New York, 1912) [Oxford University Press Edition].

## works on Spenser

Bennett, Josephine Waters, *The Evolution of "The Faerie Queene"* (Chicago, 1942; New York, 1960).

Bradner, L., *Edmund Spenser and "The Faerie Queene"* (Chicago, 1948).

Jones, H. S. V., *A Spenser Handbook* (New York, 1930).

Mueller, W. R., and D. C. Allen, eds., *"That Soueraine Light": Essays in Honor of Edmund Spenser, 1552–1952* (Baltimore, 1953).

Nelson, William, *The Poetry of Edmund Spenser* (New York, 1963) [best up-to-date treatment of Spenser's work as a whole; also available in paperback.]

Renwick, W. L., *Edmund Spenser: An Essay on Renaissance Poetry* (London, 1925) [also available in paperback].

Whitaker, Virgil K., *The Religious Basis of Spenser's Thought* (Stanford, 1950).

*The study of Spenser is in a state of rapid change and development. Among recent books which have attracted attention (but in some cases have aroused strong disagreement) are the following:*

Berger, Harry, Jr., *The Allegorical Temper: Vision and Reality in Book II of Spenser's "Faerie Queene"* (New Haven, 1957).

Cheney, Donald, *Spenser's Image of Nature in "The Faerie Queene"* (New Haven, 1966).

Ellrodt, Robert, *Neoplatonism in the Poetry of Spenser* (Geneva, 1960).

Fowler, Alastair, *Spenser and the Numbers of Time* (London, 1964).

Hamilton, A. C., *The Structure of Allegory in "The Faerie Queene"* (Oxford, 1961).

Hieatt, A. Kent, *Short Time's Endless Monument: The Symbolism of the Numbers in . . . "Epithalamion"* (New York, 1960).

Hough, Graham, *A Preface to The Faerie Queene* (London, 1962).

Lewis, C. S., *Spenser's Images of Life*, ed. A. Fowler (Cambridge, Eng., 1967).

Nelson, William, ed., *Form and Convention in the Poetry of Edmund Spenser* (Selected Papers from the English Institute, New York, 1961).

Roche, Thomas P., Jr., *The Kindly Flame: A Study of the Third and Fourth Books of Spenser's Faerie Queene* (Princeton, 1964).

Williams, Kathleen, *Spenser's Faerie Queene: the World of Glass* (London, 1966).

## background

Avery, Catherine B., *The New Century Classical Handbook* (New York, 1962).

Bush, Douglas, *Mythology and the Renaissance Tradition* (Minneapolis, 1932; New York, 1963) [available in paperback].

Harvey, Paul, *The Oxford Companion to Classical Literature* (Oxford, 1937) [frequently reprinted with corrections].

Lewis, C. S., *The Allegory of Love* (Oxford, 1936) [also available in paperback].

———, *The Discarded Image* (Cambridge, Eng., 1964).

Seznec, J., *The Survival of the Pagan Gods* (New York, 1961) [English translation].

Smith, Hallet, *Elizabethan Poetry: A Study in Convention, Meaning, and Expression* (Cambridge, Mass., 1952).

Wind, Edgar, *Pagan Mysteries in the Renaissance* (New Haven, 1958).